BECOMING AN APOSTLE OF LIGHT OF THE IMMACULATE HEART OF MARY

I0149288

Becoming an Apostle of Light of the Immaculate Heart of Mary

———

A Spirituality Based on Total Consecration to Jesus, Through Mary, In the Spirit of Saint Joseph

JAYSON M. BRUNELLE, M.Ed., CAGS

ISBN-13: 978-0692100820

ISBN-10: 0692100822

Published by
Marian Publishing
Coventry, CT
Email: jmbrunelle@marianapostolate.com
www.MarianApostolate.com

Printed in the United States of America

CONTENTS

DEDICATION

To the three most wonderful women in my life:
Firstly, to my Spiritual Mother and Mystical Spouse,
the Ever Blessed Virgin Mary, whose slave,
possession and property I am, without reservation, to
whom I literally owe my continued existence on this
earth, and my eternal salvation, should I be so
fortunate to obtain it;
Secondly, to my rock, confidante, dearest friend and
true soul-mate, Jacqueline Marie Brunelle,
my beloved wife of five years this June 7th,
without whom nothing I've done since the age of 30
would ever have transpired; and finally,
to my dear mother,
who possessed the courage to let her children make
their mistakes, that they might learn from them.

CHAPTER ONE

THE PURPOSE OF THIS BOOK

Marian Apostolate of the Laity is a web-based apostolate, dedicated to spreading the Good News of the Gospel of Christ Jesus, with an emphasis on the truly marvelous and entirely unique role that is played by the Blessed Virgin Mary, Mother of Jesus and Spiritual Mother of humanity. Through her singular cooperation in the deeply inter-connected Christological mysteries of the Incarnation and Redemption, Mary participates with Christ in His Redemptive mission. This can be best understood by looking to St. Paul's epistle to the Colossians, chapter 1, verse 24, where he states, "I rejoice in my sufferings for your sake, and fill up on my part that which is lacking of the afflictions of Christ in my flesh for his body's sake, which is the church."

Clearly, St. Paul has no intention of stating that Christ's perfectly redemptive act of complete self-sacrifice was, in some manner, lacking in it's sufficiency, for, as the Eternal Word of God, Consubstantial with the Father, nothing whatever could possibly be "lacking" in His perfect, once-for-all redemptive act. From a soteriological vantage point, Christ, as the God-man, is the only being who can offer just compensation for the infinite offenses that are committed against the infinite God. No number of finite beings, not even one so exalted in grace, merit and virtue, as the Blessed Virgin Mother of Jesus, would ever be capable of offering just compensation for the infinite offense against God that is the result of a single mortal sin.

Instead, St. Paul is referring to the opportunity that Christ has made available to each of us, the baptized members of His Mystical Body, the Church. For, if Christ has desired to make us sharers, or participants, in the salvific work of the redemption, through the exercise of the common, royal priesthood of all the baptized, how much more would this reality pertain to the Mother of God, who is, quite literally, "full of Grace," never having been touched or tainted by the least stain of original or personal sin!

Thus, we begin to realize that we are all called to be co-redeemers with Christ through the exercise of the Royal Priesthood of all the Baptized. We accomplish this chiefly through our full and active participation in the Eucharistic Liturgy, whereby we offer ourselves and the spiritual sacrifice of all the prayers, works, and sufferings of our entire lives, through, with and in Christ's perfect offering of Himself, as Priest and Victim, to the glory of God the Father.

Thus, not only does Holy Mother Church ascribe to Mary the exalted role and title of Co-Redemptrix with Christ, but also Mediatrix of all Grace; for, does it not stand to reason that she who participated with Christ in obtaining more grace for the human family than all other saints and angels combined would additionally participate in the distribution of that same grace?

Thus, it the intention and goal of this author to prove to all readers the absolute veracity of this official doctrine of the Church. For, despite wide-spread confusion regarding Mary's proper roles and titles- even amongst bishops and cardinals! – it is an absolute truth and doctrine taught by the Ordinary Magisterium of the Church that Mary is, in fact, the Mediatrix, or Dispensatrix, of every grace that comes to us, the members of Christ's mystical body, from Christ, the "Head" of that same body. Thus, the Church Fathers referred to Mary as the "neck" of the Mystical Body; for, it is precisely through the neck that all communication takes place between the Head and the Body.

It is essential that this role of Mary as Mediatrix of all Graces be properly understood, as it serves as the firm theological foundation for the tremendously sanctifying devotion of Total Consecration to Jesus through Mary. For, as the great St. Louis Marie Grignion De Montfort states, in his famed *Treatise on the True Devotion to the Blessed Virgin*,

"As our whole perfection consists in being

conformed, united and consecrated to Jesus Christ, it follows that the most perfect of all devotions is clearly the one which conforms, unites and consecrates us most perfectly to Jesus Christ. Now, as Mary is of all creatures the most conformed to Jesus Christ, it follows that of all devotions, the one that most consecrates and conforms a soul to Our Lord is the devotion to the Blessed Virgin, His Holy Mother, and that the more a soul is consecrated to Mary, the more will it be consecrated to Jesus Christ" (Treatise on True Devotion, para. 120).

While explaining and raising awareness of Mary's essential and proper roles and titles is the principle objective, or goal, of Marian Apostolate of the Laity, there is, in reality, the over-arching mission of re-evangelizing all persons with whom we come into contact, for, it is fairly evident to this author that the insidious toxins of theoretical and practical atheism have crept into virtually every aspect of our culture, to the point that intrinsic evils are viewed and pursued as goods, while authentic goodness and virtue is seen as the greatest of all evils. I cannot count how many times I have heard various persons attempting to make the argument that religion is the single greatest evil in the world, and that all war, all strife and, ultimately, every social evil conceivable can be traced back to, or has its origins in, organized religion, in general, and Catholic Christianity, in particular.

Thus, the purposes and objectives of Marian Apostolate of the Laity are as follows:

4

BECOMING AN APOSTLE OF LIGHT OF THE IMMACULATE HEART OF MARY

(1) To heed the great mandate of Christ Jesus to "Go, therefore, and make disciples of all the nations" by spreading the Gospel, or the "good news," of the Lord Jesus Christ, the Eternal Word and Only Begotten Son of the Father;

(2) To educate individuals concerning the fundamental tenets of the Catholic Christian faith, as articulated by the Magisterium, the official teaching body of the Church founded by Christ;

(3) To promote devotion to, and to educate individuals regarding, the centrality of the Holy Sacrifice of the Mass and the real, substantial and abiding presence of Christ – Body, Blood, Soul and Divinity – in the Most Holy Eucharist, which truly is – or ought to be - the "source and summit," or the "fount and apex," of our entire lives as Christians;

(4) To promulgate a theologically sound, Christocentric devotion to Mary Immaculate, Mother of Jesus Christ and our Spiritual Mother, through the spreading of the sublime devotion of Total Consecration to Mary as the perfect means of attaining transforming union with Christ;

(5) To encourage the faithful to both pray and petition for the solemn dogmatic definition of Mary as Spiritual Mother of all humanity according to her three-fold function as *Co-redemptrix* with Christ, *Mediatrix* of All Graces and *Advocate* for the People of God. Such a dogmatic definition by the Holy Father, at this critical point in the history of humanity, shall

serve as humanity's collective "*fiat*" to the Mother of God, and shall enable, or "free," her to fully exercise her role as Mediatrix of all Grace. This shall result in a tremendous, unprecedented outpouring of Mary's Divine Spouse, the Holy Spirit, upon the Church and all of humanity, and shall pave the way for the promised "Triumph of the Immaculate Heart of Mary" and the subsequent era of peace, which Our Lady has promised us at Fatima;

(6) To provide vital information concerning these, the latter-times, and the confluence of current global events and affairs, including both man-made and natural cataclysms that are being permitted by God for the sake of the purification of the Church and the world of its sinfulness, in preparation for the above-mentioned coming of a new era of holiness and authentic peace heretofore unknown. This shall constitute the coming of the "New Jerusalem" spoken of in the Book of Revelation, or the establishment of God's Kingdom on earth, whereby Christ will establish His glorious Eucharistic Reign in our midst and all of creation shall return to the perfect glorification of God. All of this will be the result of the promised "Triumph of the Immaculate Heart of Mary" in the world, to fulfill the prophetic messages dictated to the three shepherd children of Fatima in 1917; and lastly...

(7) To invite all souls who have been led to this particular apostolate by the Spirit to imitate His perfect example by "espousing" Mary's Immaculate Heart via a unique, total and complete consecration to her. Taking St. Joseph as the exemplar of one who is

perfectly consecrated to the Heart of Jesus through his perfect, spousal union with, and consecration to, the Immaculate Heart of Mary, we too, as *Apostles of Light of the Immaculate Heart*, solemnly make and live our consecration to the Heart of Mary on a daily basis, allowing Our Lady to give birth to the image and likeness of Christ in our souls. To learn more about becoming an *Apostle of Light of the Immaculate Heart of Mary*, please read on to Chapter 2.

Church-Approved Marian Apparitions and Private Revelations

Furthermore, due to the explosion of Marian apparitions on every continent and in virtually every country, this apostolate, through its website (www.MarianApostolate.com) shall address the contents of the messages given to the many visionaries and mystics who are reporting these experiences. It is the opinion of this author that we are living in the "Age of Mary," a time of grace, mercy and numerous supernatural events, a time for conversion in preparation for impending chastisements through which the world will be purified and renewed. Some of these calamities or chastisements are provisional and may be averted through prayer, fasting and penance, and may only come if the Heavenly Father's demand for penance is not satisfied. This "purification" will serve to purify and prepare the Church and the world for the promised "Triumph of the Immaculate Heart of Mary," to be followed by a new "springtime," a new era of peace and holiness for the Church and the world. Hence, the Blessed Mother's messages are ultimately messages of hope and expectation. Thus, let us boldly exclaim, "Maranatha!" – "Come, Lord Jesus!"

Mary's Messages to Humanity

The Blessed Mother has been preparing us for years through her messages to various mystics throughout the world, such as Fr. Stefano Gobbi, of the Marian Movement of Priests; the six visionaries of Medjugorje; and countless other Church-approved Marian apparitions, such as the messages of Our Lady of Akita, Japan; the myriad messages and visions given to Ida Peerdman of Amsterdam, which have received full approval by the Church, and through which the Lady of All Nations is calling upon the Church to officially and dogmatically proclaim to the Church and the world the truth of her threefold role as Co-Redemptrix, Mediatrix and Advocate. It should be noted that the miraculous events and occurrences of Akita, Japan, happened through a wooden statue of Our Lady of All Nations – the approved apparitions of Amsterdam.

It is critical that we heed the warnings of our Mother, who is calling us to prayer from the heart (specifically, the Holy Rosary), return to the daily practice of our Catholic faith which includes regular reception of the sacraments (especially daily Eucharist and monthly Confession), return to the practices of fasting, mortification, penance, the daily carrying of our cross, and the performance of the works of mercy. Most importantly, she is, through her many messages, calling us to consecrate ourselves to her Immaculate Heart, our safety and our refuge in these times of the apostasy and the widespread rejection of God and His law of Love. Of those generous souls who have entrusted their lives to Her, for her to use us up as she wishes for the greater glory of God, she is asking, above all, for prayer and suffering. She wishes to conform us into faithful replicas of Her crucified Son, and the only path that she traces out for her faithful clients is the way of the cross. For, as Christ Himself states, "Anyone who would come after me must deny his very self, pick up his cross daily, and follow me."

To encourage Christians of all states of life and of every vocation to pray and petition for the dogmatic definition of Mary as Co-Redemptrix, Mediatrix and Advocate, in order to obtain, for the Church and the world, a super-abundant outpouring of the Holy Spirit, and to pave the way for the promised "Triumph of the Immaculate Heart of Mary" in the world;

CHAPTER TWO

THE APOSTLES OF LIGHT OF
THE IMMACULATE HEART OF MARY

We, the **Apostles of Light of the Immaculate Heart of Mary,** are a spiritual society comprised of men and women of all ages and vocations – particularly the laity – who seek to live, ever more fully, the Gospel of our Lord and Redeemer, Jesus Christ – *He Who is the Way, the Truth and the Life* – and, in doing so, to proclaim and give witness, with our very lives, to the perennial veracity of the Eternal Word of God.

Further, in accord with the deeply Marian spirituality both espoused and promulgated by the great Sts. Louis Marie de Montfort, Maximilian Mary Kolbe and Pope John Paul II, we understand that this sublime vocation of a deeply "lived-out" devotion of Total Consecration to Christ Jesus, through Mary

Immaculate, is, in de Montfort's own words, "the surest, easiest, shortest, and the most perfect means" to the end of continual, ongoing sanctification, and an ever greater conformity of our will to the Divine Will.

Moreover, we have come to recognize the profound role of St. Joseph in this most sanctifying devotion of total consecration to Jesus through Mary, for Joseph, in his espousal of the Blessed Virgin Mary, becomes the perfect model of consecration to Jesus through Mary. In his espousal of our Lady, there takes place an exchange of hearts whereby Joseph offers the fullness of all that he is and all that he has to Mary, entrusting to her his heart, and Mary, who cannot and will not be outdone in liberality and generosity, meets her spouse in the same spirit, entrusting the fullness of her Immaculate Heart to him. Thus, Joseph becomes the quintessential example of one who is perfectly consecrated to Mary's Immaculate Heart.

As a purely spiritual society, the only leadership we have is that provided by the Blessed Virgin Mary herself. Thus, there exists one sole criterion for membership in this spiritual society: Full, active membership and participation in the Mystical Body of Christ, and this as witnessed to by membership in the One, Holy, Catholic and Apostolic Church of Christ Jesus, through reception of the Sacraments of Initiation (Baptism, First Holy Eucharist & Confirmation). Yet, even this criterion need not be met if one is in the process of preparation to be fully received into the Church, or even if one possesses an earnest desire to become a Catholic, and possesses the intention to initiate this process as soon as one is able.

Additionally, in the same spirit of full, filial love for, and obedience to, the Holy Magisterium of the Church (the Magisterium being comprised of the entire college of Bishops throughout world, in union with the validly elected successor of St. Peter, the Pope, who is the visible head of the Body of Christ on earth), both the *Apostles of Light of the Immaculate Heart of Mary* and *Marian Apostolate of the Laity* wish to declare our unwavering fidelity to the One, Holy, Catholic and Apostolic Church, the one Church established on the Rock of St. Peter.

It would seem appropriate, at this juncture, to address an issue which not infrequently comes up when addressing the legitimacy of *Marian Apostolate of the Laity*, and / or the *Apostles of Light of the Sacred Hearts of Jesus, Mary & Joseph* operating as "lay apostolates" within the Church. Invariably, persons will inquire whether these so-called "lay apostolates" have received any "official   recognition" from, or "approval" by the "Church," whether from the Local Ordinary (in whose diocese we operate), or from the Vatican.

In an effort to provide the most theologically and canonically sound answer to the above articulated questions, I shall here refer the reader to Chapter Four of the document, *"Apostolicam Actuositatem,"* which is *"The Decree on the Apostolate of the Laity,"* solemnly promulgated by His Holiness, Pope Paul VI, on 18 November, 1965:

"15. The laity can engage in their apostolic activity either as individuals or together as members of various groups or associations.

"16. The individual apostolate, flowing generously from its source in a truly Christian life (cf. John 4:14), is the origin and condition of the whole lay apostolate, even of the organized type, and it admits of no substitute.

"Regardless of status, all lay persons (including those who have no opportunity or possibility for collaboration in associations) are called to this type of apostolate and obliged to engage in it. This type of apostolate is useful at all times and places, but in certain circumstances it is the only one appropriate and feasible.

"There are many forms of the apostolate whereby the laity build up the Church, sanctify the world, and give it life in Christ. A particular form of the individual apostolate as well as a sign specially suited to our times is the testimony of the whole lay life arising from faith, hope, and charity.

"It manifests Christ living in those who believe in Him. Then by the apostolate the spoken and written word, which is utterly necessary under certain circumstances, lay people announce Christ, explain and spread His teaching in accordance with one's status and ability, and faithfully profess it.

"Furthermore, in collaborating as citizens of this world, in whatever pertains to the upbuilding and conducting of the temporal order, the laity must seek in the light of faith loftier motives of action in their family, professional, cultural, and social life and make them known to others when the occasion arises. Doing this, they should be aware of the fact that they are cooperating with God the creator, redeemer, and sanctifier and are giving praise to Him.

"Finally, the laity should vivify their life with charity and express it as best they can in their works.

"They should all remember that they can reach all men and contribute to the salvation of the whole world by public worship and prayer as well as by penance and voluntary acceptance of the labors and hardships of life whereby they become like the suffering Christ" (cf. 2 Cor. 4:10; Col. 1:24).

Thus, according to this author's interpretation of the above quotation, it would certainly appear that *Marian Apostolate of the Laity* and the *Apostles of Light of the Immaculate Heart of Mary* both possess the full, unequivocal approval of the Church, both local and universal.

Moreover, as so many adopted brothers and sisters of Christ, our Lord, and docile children of our Spiritual Mother, Mary Immaculate, we consider ourselves to

be of one mind, heart and body – a concrete reality
that is both expressed and brought about through our
daily reception of the Holy Eucharist and in our daily
prayer of the Holy Rosary of Our Lady. Our way of
life is based on the shared ideal of striving, with the
help of God's grace, to live the Gospel of Jesus Christ
to the letter, with a particular emphasis on:

(1) *The Holy Eucharist* (daily reception of our Lord
in the Holy Sacrifice of the Mass and the frequent
practice of Holy Hours of adoration and reparation to
the Sacred Heart of Jesus, truly and substantially
present in the Eucharistic species);

(2) *Total consecration of ourselves to the
Immaculate Heart of Mary, in the "spirit" of St.
Joseph* (with an understanding that Mary, as the
Mediatrix of all Grace, can only fully carry out this
unique and most powerful role of hers with regard to
those souls who have entirely entrusted themselves to
her, and who, in imitation of St. Joseph, unite their
hearts to hers in a profound union of unconditional,
committed love); and,

(3) A *deep love and prayer for, and an
unwavering fidelity to, the Holy Father and the
Magisterium, the teaching and governing body of
the Church on earth, who alone has been
entrusted with the task of interpreting Sacred
Scripture, and through whom the Holy Spirit
speaks to His Church and the world as the
Sacred Living Tradition of that same Church.*

JAYSON M. BRUNELLE, M.Ed., CAGS

CHAPTER THREE:

MISSION STATEMENT

In essence, the goal, or mission, of the *Apostles of Light of the Immaculate*, is to spend ourselves evermore completely, and to give of ourselves evermore generously, in cooperation with the grace of God, mediated through Mary Immaculate – Mediatrix of all Graces – in an unceasing act of adoration, glorification, gratitude, expiation, reparation and supplication to the Sacred and Eucharistic Heart of our Lord, Jesus Christ. Moreover, we offer to Mary, and place on the altar of her Immaculate Heart, all of the prayers, works, joys & sufferings of each day and of our entire lives.

Having accepted her sublime invitation to suffer martyrdom of the heart in reparation for the sins of the world, and knowing we shall find no comfort outside the safe refuge of her Immaculate Heart, to which we have entrusted all that we are and have, we turn to her as our sole comfort in the dark hour of our immolation. Miraculously, she brings it about that we begin to taste the sweetness of that deep and abiding joy of suffering for the salvation of our brothers and sisters who have lost the sense of sin, and consequently, do not repent of it.

Thus, our daily participation in the Eucharistic Liturgy is the focal point of each day and of our entire lives, for it is precisely through the sacred Liturgy that we gather around the heavenly banquet table, which, simultaneously, is the altar of sacrifice, whereupon Christ offers Himself as the perfect oblation, the spotless lamb of sacrifice, taking upon Himself the sins of humanity and making possible the reconciliation of God and man (a reconciliation which begins at the moment of the Incarnation, when Christ hypostatically reconciles His human nature with His Divine Nature in His one Divine Person). The liturgical re-presentation of Christ's once-for-all Paschal Sacrifice enables us, the members of His Mystical Body, to exercise the Royal Priesthood that was conferred upon us at the moment of our Baptism. Thus, we ask Mary to unite our spiritual sacrifices to Christ's perfect offering of Himself to the Father, in atonement for our sins and those of the whole world.

Finally, we pray that through our daily consumption of, and holy communion with, the true Body, Blood, Soul and Divinity of Our Lord in the Holy Eucharist (a term which, from the original ancient Greek, means "thanksgiving"), Christ might fulfill His promise, such that He might live in us, and we might live in Him.

Further, if the Eucharist is to be at the center of our every day and our entire life, then it logically follows that the soul will become increasingly grateful to God for everything that God so freely, lovingly and generously gives to and shares with us. Such an "attitude of gratitude" ought to pulsate throughout every fiber of our being, literally bringing us to our knees in thanksgiving for, and awe-struck wonder at, the infinite goodness of God. Thus, we are compelled to permit Christ to live, work, pray and suffer again in each of us, the members of His Mystical Body. In so doing, He will shine the Divine Light of His Love, Peace, Joy, Truth and Goodness through us, and onto all persons with whom we come into contact. And, since Mary is the true Mediatrix and Advocate between Christ and humanity, His divine light must first pass through Mary's Maternal and Immaculate Heart, where it takes on the distinct shape, color and dimensions of the Heart of a Mother – our one, Immaculate Mother Mary.

Thus, as Apostles of Light of the Immaculate, we spread, all about us, the Light of Christ, which passes through the Heart of Mary, the first and most perfect Apostle of Light.

To Become an Apostle of Light of the Immaculate:

- Make a nine-day preparation for your Total Consecration to Mary. Your preparation should begin exactly nine days prior to a significant <u>Marian Feast Day</u> or <u>Solemnity</u>.

- On the ninth and last day, make a good confession, participate in the Holy Sacrifice of the Mass, receive Our Lord in Holy Communion, and after Mass, kneel at the foot of the Tabernacle and recite, with a humble heart, clear intention and deliberation, the prayer of <u>Total Consecration of the Apostles of Light of the Immaculate</u>.
- Become invested in the <u>Brown Scapular</u> of Our Lady of Mt. Carmel, wear the scapular devoutly each day of your life, and ask the priest who invests you for permission to substitute the daily prayer of five decades of the Holy Rosary of Our Lady in place of the daily prayer of the "Little Office of the Blessed Virgin Mary." In doing so, you shall be admitted to the spiritual benefits of the entire Carmelite Order.
- Pray at least the five decades of the Holy Rosary that you have promised to pray to Our Lady of Mt. Carmel, in association with the wearing of her garment, the Holy Scapular. Further, enroll yourself in the <u>Rosary Confraternity of the Dominican Fathers</u>. In doing so, you shall participate in the spiritual benefits of the entire Dominican Order.
- Make every effort to attend Mass daily, or at least as often as possible – your daily duties permitting.
- Enroll yourself in the <u>Association of the Miraculous Medal</u> and enroll at least 12 persons each year. In doing so, you shall become a promoter of the Miraculous Medal, and shall receive, in addition to the spiritual

benefits of being a promoter, the Apostolic
Blessing of the Holy Father. The cost is
nominal – a mere 25 cents per person. Thus,
it will cost you only three dollars to enroll
twelve persons each year; remember to renew
this enrollment each 12 months. Moreover,
be sure to wear your Miraculous Medal
around your neck, visibly, as an outward sign
of your interior disposition of heart.

- Enroll yourself in the <u>Militia Immaculata</u> of
St. Maximilian Kolbe.
- Set aside at least 15 minutes per day for Lectio
Divina (spiritual reading). You may read
<u>Sacred Scripture</u>; <u>"True Devotion to Mary,"
by St. Louis de Montfort</u>; the <u>"Summa
Theologia" of St. Thomas Aquinas</u>; the 1917
edition of <u>"The Catholic Encyclopedia;"</u> any
of the theologically rich Documents of the
Second Vatican Council, such as <u>Lumen
Gentium</u>, <u>Gaudiem et Spes</u>, <u>Dei Verbum</u> or
<u>Sacrosanctum Concilium</u>; the <u>Catechism of
the Catholic Church</u>, or any of numerous
writings of the <u>Early Church Fathers,</u> such as
the writings of St. Ambrose, St. Athanasius,
St. Augustine, St. Basil the Great, St. Cyril of
Jerusalem, St. Ephraim the Syrian, Pope St.
Gregory the Great, St. Gregory Nazianzen, St.
Hilary of Poitiers, St. Jerome, St. John of
Damascus, St. John Chrysostom or Pope St.
Leo the Great, all of whom are not only great
saints, but additionally have been designated
as "Doctors" of the Church" – the single
highest honor that can be bestowed upon any

canonized saint of the Church. All of the above mentioned documents are freely available to you online, or via your smartphone via great Catholic Apps like Laudate, the IPieta series, New Advent, IBreviary, et cetera.

▪ Pray, on a daily basis, that our Lady will clothe you with her own virtues of Faith, Hope, Charity, Purity, Temperance, Fortitude, Humility, Poverty of Spirit, Spiritual Childhood, all the graces necessary to cooperate fully and completely with the Divine Will of God the Father at each moment of your life, and the grace to be fully attentive to the promptings and movements of the Spirit within your soul.

▪ Exercise, as often as opportunities present themselves, the corporeal and spiritual works of mercy; for, we shall only be shown mercy to the extent that we, ourselves, have shown mercy.

▪ Plead with our Lord and our Lady to rid you of all self-love, all egoism, all self-pre-occupation, all narcissism, all selfishness, and pray daily the Litany of Humility by Cardinal Merry del Val. Beg the Three Hearts of Jesus, Mary & Joseph to free you of the self-centered desires to be accepted, to be loved, to be esteemed, to be remembered, to be thought well of, to be consulted, etc. Beg to be freed of the self-centered fears of being rejected, being despised, suffering rebukes, being suspected, being calumniated, being falsely accused, being humiliated, and so on.

Pray for the grace to sincerely desire that others may be more esteemed than you, that, in the opinion of the world, others may increase and that you may decrease; that others may be praised while you go unnoticed; that others may be chosen while you are set aside, and that others become holier than you, provided that you become as holy as you should, in accordance with God's Providence and His most holy and Divine Will. This is the goal of everything outlined above. This is that radical littleness to which you have been called by your Heavenly Mother, should you choose to second her plan for you, your soul, and the souls that have been entrusted to your care and prayer; for, as it has many times been said: "The salvation of the many depends on the sanctification of the few," and, "Many are called, yet few are chosen."

CHAPTER FOUR

THEOLOGY OF MARIAN CONSECRATION

As Christians, we take Christ as the exemplar of how to live as adopted sons and daughters of God the Father. We understand that it behooves us to imitate Christ in each of the mysteries of His life on earth, for, Christ is "the Way" to the Father. Moreover, Holy Mother Church, founded by Christ on the "rock" of the apostle Peter, teaches that there exists a certain "hierarchy" of divinely revealed truths and mysteries of the holy faith. Among these truths, the two most important and fundamental mysteries of our Christian faith are (1) the mystery of the Holy Trinity; and (2) the mystery of Christ's Incarnation.

If, as Christians, we are to imitate Christ, our Lord, in each of the mysteries of His life, and if the

Incarnation of the Word in the virginal womb of Mary is among the most important and fundamental of all Christian mysteries and truths, then it logically follows that we should imitate our Lord, Who became a little child and entrusted Himself entirely and unreservedly to the care of His Mother, Mary. Should not we, too, as followers of Christ, the Way, imitate the action of our Savior by becoming like children and entrusting ourselves unreservedly to the care of Mary, who, in addition to being the Mother of Christ, is simultaneously and necessarily the true Spiritual Mother of the Mystical Body, the Church, which cannot be separated from Christ, its head?

Moreover, the Logos, the Second Person of the Most Holy Trinity, could have chosen any means whatsoever to enter into the earthly realm of space and time; but of all possible means, He chose Mary. If Christ, Who, as God, could have chosen an infinite number of ways to come to meet humanity, decided upon Mary as the most illustrious pathway by which to meet humanity, should this not serve as the single greatest reason for us, His disciples, to imitate our Lord in choosing Mary as the most sublime of all pathways by which to return to Him?

In short, Jesus chose to unite the Immaculate Heart of His Mother Mary most perfectly with His own Sacred Heart and to share His perfect redemptive and salvific mission with her. It is for this reason that Mary is called the Co-Redemptrix, Mediatrix of all grace and Advocate for the People of God. These three roles of Mary best express Mary's Spiritual

Motherhood of all humanity in the order of Grace. For, she who gave birth to Christ, the source of all grace and mercy, can certainly be said to be the Mother of all who benefit from that grace and mercy. Moreover, it was from the Altar of the Cross that the dying Jesus entrusted His Most Holy Mother to all of humanity, represented by the beloved apostle John, when, from the Cross of our Salvation, Christ stated, "Woman, behold thy son....Behold thy mother" (Jn 19:26).

This brings us to the sound theological foundation upon which Marian Consecration rests: Mary's true function as Spiritual Mother of all humanity, expressed according to her three-fold function as Co-Redemptrix, Mediatrix of all grace, and Advocate for the People of God. Let us, then, explore the first two of these three aspects of Mary's Spiritual Motherhood, in order to better understand the logic and necessity of Consecration to Mary, our Spiritual Mother.

Mary as Co-Redemptrix

The following ideas derive from the writings of the early Church Fathers, who identified Jesus as the "New Adam," and Mary, His Most Holy Mother, as the "New Eve." Just as the first Eve provided the first Adam with the fruit as the instrument of the fall, in like fashion does Mary, the "New Eve," provide Jesus, the "New Adam," with his body as the instrument of the Redemption.

Mary, or the "Woman," is spoken of at the very

beginning of Sacred Scripture, in Genesis 3:15, and at
the very end of Sacred Scripture, in Revelation 12:1.
In both instances, this "Woman," which, incidentally,
is the precise phraseology used by Jesus in referring
to His Mother Mary all throughout the four Gospels,
is portrayed as the archenemy of the Devil, or Satan.
In Genesis, 3:15, we read: "I will put enmities
between thee and the woman, and thy seed and her
seed: she shall crush thy head, and thou shalt lie in
wait for her heel." This passage, referred to by
theologians as the "Proto-Evangelium," or the "First
Gospel," depicts God the Father's first promise of
salvation, redemption and restoration for a humanity
which, having been seduced by Satan, severed four
fundamental relationships as a consequence of the
original fall. The four relationships that were either
severed or significantly impaired were: (1) man's
relationship with God, resulting in the deprivation of
sanctifying grace, or the lack of the indwelling
presence of the Holy Spirit as the soul of man's soul;
(2) man's relationship with himself, or man's inability
to subject his passions/emotions to right reasoning,
an internal conflict referred to by theologians as
concupiscence; (3) man's relationship with other men,
such that in place of a spirit of cooperation with and
concern for one's neighbor, there exists, instead, a
desire to dominate and manipulate the other, who is
now regarded as a "stranger" to be feared and an
"enemy" to be overcome; and lastly, (4) man's
relationship with nature itself, which, prior to the fall,
posed no threat to the well-being of man, but, as a
consequence of the fall, has introduced pain, suffering
and death into the lives of men.

Gratefully, the Sacrament of Baptism restores man to God's friendship, allowing for the indwelling presence of the Holy Spirit of God in the soul of Man. Yet, the Scripture passages quoted above make clear that the salvific action of Christ, whereby humanity would be restored to God the Father's friendship and "good graces," would be intimately associated with this "Woman." Jesus, the "Word of God," refers to himself as the "Alpha and Omega, the beginning and the end" (Rev 1:8). Mary, the "Woman" of Scripture, appears at "the beginning and the end" of the "Word of God." Thus, it is manifestly clear to this author that God had Mary, "the glory of Jerusalem...the great pride of Israel...the highest honor of our people" (Judith 15:10), in mind well before the creation of the world; for, it was in accord with His Holy and Divine Will that the Savior of Humanity, the Second Person of the Holy Trinity, would graft a true human nature to His Divine Person, and that the "Woman" from whom the God-man's sinless human nature would come would, herself, be without the least stain of original sin, "blessed...by God Most High, beyond all women on earth" (Judith 13:23), and, for that very reason, would cooperate in a wholly singular and unique fashion with her Divine Son in the defeat of Satan not once, but twice: that is, she would precede both the first and second comings of Christ. Mary was the immaculate gateway through which Christ, the Son of God, entered into the world in a most humble and obscure fashion approximately 2,000 years ago. In His first coming, His divinity was overshadowed and hidden by His humanity. Now, in our times, Mary is once again preparing the world for the Second Coming of her divine Son; only this time, his humanity shall be obscured and overshadowed by his glorious divinity. Both of Christ's comings herald a great victory for God, Mary and each of their faithful children that coincides with a great defeat of Satan. Such was the case in Christ's first coming, and so shall it be in His glorious Second Coming, which, if one knows how to read the signs of the times, is on the verge of taking place.

Thus, the "Woman" who begins and ends Sacred Scripture, the "Woman" who preceded the first coming of Christ and participated in a wholly unique and singular fashion in His victorious defeat of Satan, sin and death, is again preceding His second Glorious coming through her numerous apparitions all over the globe. She is preparing her faithful and victorious cohort of children who shall entrust themselves unreservedly to her, that they might be thoroughly imbued with her spirit and truly make up the Apostles of Light of the Immaculate Heart, in order to afford Christ, her divine Son, the greatest possible glorification. These children of Mary comprise the humble "heel" of the Mystical body of Christ, that shall definitively crush the head of the ancient serpent. Moreover, they, in imitation of their Most Holy Queen, offer themselves, their prayers and especially their sufferings through, with and in Christ to the glory of God the Father and for the salvation of souls.

This is not to say that there is anything whatever lacking in the perfect redemptive act of Christ.

Instead, it has pleased Christ to associate his adopted sisters and brothers, His co-heirs of the Kingdom, in his ongoing work of redemption. And Mary takes first place among the Co-redeemers with Christ, becoming the Co-Redemptrix. For, if St. Paul, among the greatest of Evangelists in the history of the Church, could state, "Now I rejoice in my sufferings for your sake, and fill up on my part that which is lacking of the afflictions of Christ in my flesh for his body's sake, which is the church," how much more should this apply to Mary, who, unlike St. Paul, was wholly untouched by the least taint of sin? It should be noted, however, for the sake of theological accuracy, and to avoid any confusion, that Mary's participation in the work of Redemption is wholly subordinate to and dependent upon Christ's perfect salvific act of redemption on Calvary. Nevertheless, it has pleased the Godhead to afford Mary a unique participation in the economy of salvation. Furthermore, you and I have been called to participate in the marvelous, ongoing work of the redemption. This we do by exercising the royal, common priesthood that was bestowed upon us at our Baptism. The People of God are a Priestly People. This is to say that through our baptism into Christ's Mystical Body, we were made participants in the priestly, prophetic and kingly offices of Christ, the One Eternal High Priest. Thus, in addition to the ministerial priesthood which is bestowed upon men who receive the Sacrament of Holy Orders, there exists the Common, Royal Priesthood of all baptized believers.

We, the members of Christ's Royal Priesthood,

properly exercise this function by assisting at Holy
Mass and by living the Mass. Thus, the exercise of
our royal priesthood is contingent upon the exercise
of the Ministerial Priesthood. While these two
participations in the one priesthood of Christ differ
not only in degree but also in essence, it is by no
means any less dignified to offer oneself as an
oblation on the altar of Mary's Immaculate Heart as a
lay person. Rather, this constitutes the truly sublime
and exalted vocation to which each of the baptized
members of Christ's Mystical Body has been called.
We exercise our Royal Priesthood by participating in
the Holy Sacrifice of the Mass, whereby Christ
continues His work of redemption through, with and
in us, as a consequence of our reception of His Most
Precious Body and Blood in the Holy Eucharist. For,
as Christ states in the Gospel of John, "He who eats
My flesh and drinks My blood abides in Me, and I in
him" (Jn 6:56).

Mary's role as Co-Redemptrix began at the moment
of the Incarnation, when she provided the Only
begotten Son of the Father, the Eternal Word of
God, with his human body and nature, which He
forever grafted to His Divine Nature, in what is
referred to as the Hypostasis. Thus, Christ's work of
Redemption began at the moment of the Incarnation,
where He reconciled, in His one Divine Person,
humanity and divinity. Thus, it is entirely
theologically correct to state that the start of the work
of Redemption would never have taken place without
Mary's full consent and unconditional cooperation
with the Divine Will of the Father, who freely chose

to become dependent upon her fiat. Moreover, it is additionally at the moment of the Incarnation that Mary begins her role as Spiritual Mother of all of humanity; for, in giving birth to Christ, the Head, she simultaneously and necessarily gives birth to the body connected to that Head, which is the Church. Ultimately, Mary's role as Co-Redemptrix is brought to completion at the foot of the cross, where Mary mystically participated in the sufferings of Christ, consenting to the immolation of this victim Who was her dearly beloved Son and Savior. Her maternal suffering was so intense that she merited more grace than any other creature. Finally, it was precisely at the foot of the Cross that Christ designated Mary as the Spiritual Mother of all humanity, for it was there that she, in an unprecedented and unmatched fashion, participated with her Son in meriting grace and mercy, or divine life, for the human family. It is for this reason, then, that Mary is rightly termed the Co-Redemptrix; for, as was stated earlier, if Saint Paul, in speaking about his own sufferings, could state, "Now I rejoice in my sufferings for your sake, and fill up on my part that which is lacking of the afflictions of Christ in my flesh for his body's sake, which is the church" (Col 1:24), how much more should this apply to the Blessed Virgin Mary, who never knew sin and was wholly Immaculate from the first moment of her conception?

Mary as Mediatrix of all Grace

While the first dimension of Mary's Spiritual Motherhood is carried out through her Co-redemptive participation with her divine Son in the meriting of grace and mercy, or divine life, for humanity (in a manner that is entirely dependant upon and subordinate to Christ's perfect Redemptive act), Mary's role as the Mediatrix of all grace is the logical continuation of this Spiritual Motherhood. As any good mother will tell you, motherhood certainly does not cease with the definitive act of giving birth, but instead continues in the nourishing and nurturing of the child long after it has been born until such time as the child reaches full maturation. The same must be said of the Blessed Virgin with regard to the nourishing and nurturing of the spiritual children that she participated with Christ in giving birth to. As Co-Redemptrix, Mary participates with Christ in giving birth to the Church, whose Sacramental life gushes forth from the pierced Heart of Christ. Indeed, we might state that the Sacramental life of the Church was additionally born of the Heart of Mary, whose Heart, perfectly united as it is with her Son's, was also necessarily pierced, in fulfillment of the prophecy of Simeon: "Indeed, a sword will pierce your own soul, too, so that the inner thoughts of many people might be revealed" (Lk 2:35). Further, it is fitting that she, who participated with Christ in the meriting of grace, continue to exercise her maternal function by participating in the mediation and distribution of that grace.

Thus, each of the Divine Persons of the Trinity has freely chosen to associate Mary, the "Woman" who begins and ends divine revelation, in every aspect of the economy of salvation: God the Father freely chose to become dependent upon Mary's fiat in her acceptance of His invitation to become the Theotokos; God the Son freely chose to become dependent upon Mary by emptying Himself of His divinity, becoming an infant, and entrusting himself entirely and without reserve to the maternal care of Mary; God the Holy Spirit, the true spouse of the Blessed Virgin Mary, has freely chosen to become dependent upon Mary's Maternal Mediation in the distribution of all graces that spring from the bosom of the Father, are merited or purchased with the Blood of Christ, and are distributed by the Holy Spirit. The Holy Spirit, like the other two Divine Persons, has also freely chosen to act solely through, with and in Mary. Thus, the Church's official doctrine concerning Mary's role as Mediatrix of all graces is that nothing of the vast treasury of God's grace comes to us but through the willed intercession of the Blessed Virgin Mary. Thus, every gift of grace from God to humanity is additionally a gift of the Mother.

The great St. Louis Marie de Montfort explains that when it comes to the distribution of God's grace, Mary truly distributes this grace to whom she wills, to the extent that she wills, in the manner that she wills. This may sound extreme to some; yet the precedent for this has been set in Sacred Scripture itself. For, in John's Gospel account of the feast of the Wedding at Cana, we read the following exchange taking place between Jesus and His Mother: "When the wine was gone, Jesus' mother said to him, 'They have no more wine.' 'Dear woman, why do you involve me?' Jesus replied. 'My time has not yet come.' His mother said to the servants, 'Do whatever he tells you'" (Jn 2:3-5).

In this passage, Jesus makes it quite clear to Mary that
He has no intention of performing a miracle, indeed,
his first "public" miracle, on that particular occasion.
Yet, as we read on, Jesus does, in fact, perform His
first public miracle, turning water into wine. The
conversation that takes place between Jesus and His
Mother Mary manifests the tremendous influence
Mary has on her Son. In short, as the saints never tire
of stating, "Christ simply cannot refuse His Most
Holy Mother." Thus, in the Gospel account of the
Wedding at Cana, we catch a glimpse into the
tremendous intercessory power of Mary, and God's
inability to refuse a plea from His Most Holy Mother
on our behalf. Indeed, how good shall it go for us at
the pivotal moment of our particular judgment should
we secure Mary's intercession and Advocacy, which
she promises to those who exercise true devotion to
her through the daily prayer of the Holy Rosary.

Papal Pronouncements Concerning Mary's True Function as Mediatrix of All Grace

There is no question that Vatican II, and the 16
documents that issued therefrom, were truly a gift
from God to the Church, manifesting the very real
action of the Spirit of God working in and through
the Council Fathers. This gathering of all the world's
bishops, working in union with the popes who
headed the Council, was, for the world, a concrete
example of Sacred Tradition in action. And while
Mary, the Mother of God, was certainly given special
attention by the Council, as there had been
discussions amongst the bishops of a dogmatic

definition of Mary's Co-redemption, Mediation and Advocacy, as well as the dedication of the entirety of Chapter 8 of *Lumen Gentium*, the Dogmatic Constitution on the Church, to the preeminent role of the Blessed Virgin Mary in the life of the Church, we additionally know that there were, indeed, a certain number of bishops who were significantly opposed to these particular Marian titles. These latter, in an effort to foster ecumenical dialogue with representatives of the various Protestant denominations, whom the Church had invited to participate in the Conciliar proceedings as "observers", believed that, despite numerous previous Papal and Magisterial teachings and official pronouncements regarding Mary's true roles as Co-redemptrix and Mediatrix of all grace, these particular Marian titles, whilst comprising Marian truths belonging to the Sacred deposit of Faith, should be avoided so as not to impede ecumenical efforts by fostering or arousing theological confusion.

Thus, to this day, there exist two schools of thought regarding this issue. On the one hand, there are those theologians who oppose a dogmatic definition of these three roles that comprise the exercise of Mary's Spiritual Motherhood of humanity, believing that such a pronouncement would harm ecumenical efforts. On the other hand, there are those theologians, such as the author of this article, who fully support and endorse the dogmatic definition of Mary's roles as Co-redemptrix, Mediatrix and Advocate, believing that, contrary to being harmful to ecumenism, a solemn Papal definition of Mary's Spiritual Motherhood according to these three functions would, in effect, constitute humanity's collective fiat to Mary's Maternal Mediation, thereby "freeing" the Blessed Virgin to fully exercise her Maternal Mediation for both the Church and the world, obtaining for these latter a super-abundant, profound outpouring of the grace and mercy of the Holy Spirit, her well-beloved Divine Spouse, upon all of humanity, thereby resulting in a new, second Pentecost, which would most assuredly foster an authentic ecumenism that doesn't resort to a watering down of the Sacred Truths of our Holy Catholic faith.

We must recall one of the most basic and fundamental axioms of moral theology; namely, that the *end* never justifies the *means*. In this instance, the end, or goal, would be a greater unification amongst the various Christian denominations, a most necessary goal for which Christ, Himself, prayed. Yet, in our efforts to bring about such a unity amongst Christians, it is never permissible to sacrifice, "water-down" or "discard" authentic and divinely revealed truths of the Sacred Deposit of Faith.

Regarding the numerous Papal pronouncements concerning the veracity of Mary's role as Mediatrix of all grace, Fr. Alessandro M. Apollonio F.I. has done us a marvelous service in collecting and assembling salient quotations from numerous pontiffs that underscore, in no uncertain terms, the absolute truth of Mary's undeniable role as the Mediatrix of all grace after Christ, the sole Mediator between humanity and the Eternal Father. In his article, *Mary Mediatrix of All Graces, Part II*, Fr. Apollonio provides a comprehensive list of the many Papal statements that have been made affirming Mary's true role as Mediatrix of all grace. To view this most impressive display of Papal and Magisterial pronouncements regarding Mary's true function as Mediatrix, please see the article below.

Thus, as Fr. Apollonio illustrates in the article below, *"Mary's universal mediation has been the object of the unchanging ordinary Papal Magisterium for at least the past three centuries and therefore must be considered Catholic doctrine, definitive tenenda, not dogmatically defined, but certainly definable."*

Mary's Role as Mediatrix of All Graces Provides the Theological Foundation for Marian Consecration

Let us clearly state from the outset that all authentic, theologically sound devotion to the Mother of God is necessarily and entirely Christocentric. This is to say that all devotion to Mary, the Mother of God and our Mother, must always be understood to be a means to the end of a more perfect and profound devotion to and transforming union with the Sacred Heart of Christ. Catholics have often been accused by their Protestant brethren of "Mariolotry," or rendering the worship that is due to God alone, to Mary. If it ever has happened (although such a situation would more than likely be impossible, as shall later be explained) that a person were to literally engage in the "worship" of Mother Mary, this would certainly constitute idol worship, and would, indeed, be a grave violation of the first and greatest commandment, which is to love

God above all things, with one's entire heart, soul,
strength and mind.

St. Louis de Montfort, the great champion of
consecration to Jesus through Mary, clearly explains
that Mary's sole function is to lead souls ever more
perfectly to her Divine Son, and to assist, through her
most powerful intercession, in the configuration of
each soul into the image and likeness of Christ her
Son. Thus, whatsoever we give to Mary, we, of
necessity, give to Jesus. Mary in no way keeps
anything we should entrust to her for herself, as if she
were the last end of devotion to her. Instead, she is a
proximate end, or a means to the end of an ever more
perfect conformity to the Divine Will, who is literally
incapable of doing anything that would not lead souls
to an ever deeper and more profound communion
with Christ, her Son. Despite this fundamental
theological reality, there are not a few Christians who
view devotion to Mary as an obstacle to their
devotion to or union with Christ, as if devotion to
Mary somehow detracts from devotion to Christ. As
stated above, Mary's sole function is that of leading
her children to Christ. Mary's words, as recorded by
the Evangelist John, echo throughout all ages, as she
states to men and women of every generation, "Do
whatever He tells you" (Jn 2:5). She repeats these
words to Christians of all times, places and cultures,
and is, quite literally, incapable of doing otherwise.
Thus, all devotion to Mary is, of necessity, devotion
to Jesus.

Moreover, devotion to Mary perfects our devotion to

Christ, and (1) speeds us along the path of sanctity; (2) brings about a profound detachment from the world, the flesh and the devil – the three chief enemies of our souls and our eternal salvation; (3) enables us to love Christ with the perfect and immaculate love of Mary's Immaculate Heart, which has never known or been sullied by the least taint or shadow of sin.

De Montfort explains in the introduction of his Treatise on True Devotion to Mary that the goal of every Christian is to become as perfectly conformed to the image and likeness of Christ as is possible. Thus, the greatest of all devotions to Christ would be that devotion which most perfectly conforms and unites us to Christ. Now, of all creatures, the Blessed Virgin Mary, Mother of God, through the singular privileges of her Divine Maternity, Perpetual Virginity, Immaculate Conception and her glorious Assumption, is most perfectly conformed to Christ in all things, in each of the mysteries that comprise His life on earth. Ergo, it logically follows that, if the greatest of devotions is that which most perfectly unites us to Christ in all things, and if Mary, of all creatures is, indeed, most perfectly united to Christ, then the most perfect, most sanctifying and most efficacious of all devotions must be a perfect devotion to Mary. And, as de Montfort continues on, the apex of true devotion to Mary, Mother of God, is that of Total Consecration to her, whereby we renew, in her Immaculate and merciful hands and Heart, the solemn vows of our baptism, and proceed to entrust everything that we are and everything that we possess, in the orders of nature, grace and glory, to Mary, for her to dispose of according to her will, which is always perfectly conformed to the Most Holy and Divine Will of God. This, then, encapsulates the essence of the devotion of Total Consecration to Mary. For, how can a mother nourish a child who puts up resistance to her? We must be docile children in Our Mother's most merciful and loving arms, allowing ourselves to be nourished by her with the milk of divine grace.

The key idea is that Mary, like God, has a profound respect for our freewill as human persons. Certainly, her Immaculate Heart is consumed with a profound maternal love for each and every one of her children, especially those who are the furthest away from her Son, the Good Shepherd. It is the most ardent desire of her Heart, as a true Mother to humanity, to save each soul that runs the risk of eternal perdition. Yet, she simply will not force herself on any of her numerous children. Instead, we must freely invite her to take up residence in our souls, and there is no question that she will, indeed, fly to the soul that solemnly consecrates itself to her. In her apparitions to St. Catherine Laboure, who was shown the image of the Miraculous Medal and was told by Our Lady to have the medal struck according to the vision she had received, St. Catherine noticed that on the obverse of the medal, Our Lady of Grace was depicted standing on the globe, with a serpent under her feet, and from rings on Our Lady's fingers, there emanated rays of light (symbolizing grace and mercy) from some but not all of the gemstones. Our Lady described the image's symbolism: "The ball which you see represents the world...and each person in particular. These rays symbolize the graces I shed upon those who ask for them. The jewels which give no rays symbolize the graces that are not given because they are not asked for."

From this description given by Our Lady, herself, it is clear that we must exercise our freewill in petitioning Our Lady for the graces which we are in such dire need of, and which she is ever-ready to provide, if we but ask her. And it is precisely through our Act of Consecration to her Immaculate Heart and the living of that Consecration that Our Lady will remain utterly faithful to her solemn promise to provide, as our Spiritual Mother, for each and every one of our needs – both spiritual and material.

Consecration Frees Mary to Fully Exercise Her Role as Mediatrix in Souls

This brings us to the crux of our thesis: Mary is only capable of carrying out the fullness of her role as Mediatrix of all Grace with respect to those souls who have solemnly and unreservedly entrusted themselves to her maternal care and mediation through a solemn act of Total Consecration to her and the subsequent living of that Total Consecration. Thus, Mary's rightful role as Mediatrix of all Graces can only be fully exercised in those souls who have become her full possession and property. Moreover, it is not enough to simply recite a prayer of consecration to Mary; instead, we must conscientiously seek to live with Mary, through Mary, in Mary and for Mary. We must beg her, each day of our lives, to take our hearts, full of vice, iniquity, sin, defects, ingratitude, pride, attachment to ourselves and our way of thinking and feeling, and so on, and replace them with her Most Immaculate Heart; a heart that truly is "full of grace," without the least taint or shadow of sin or self-love, and that beats only and always with a pure, perfect love for God and for each one of her countless spiritual children. Thus, we can be assured of a rapid yet profound increase in personal sanctification and growth in holiness through the action of Our Holy Mother Mary in the desert of our souls when we make a solemn act of total consecration to the Most Immaculate Heart of Mary, Our Spiritual Mother, and make every effort to truly live that Consecration, which should entail (1) becoming enrolled in and continuously wearing the Brown Scapular of Our Lady of Mount Carmel, which she has referred to as the "religious habit" of those totally entrusted or consecrated to her; (2) the daily praying of at least five decades of her prayer, the Most Holy Rosary (while meditating on the Joyful, Sorrowful, Glorious or Luminous mysteries); (3) daily participation in the Holy Sacrifice of the Mass and reception of the Most Holy Eucharist, which, as has been explained in-depth in previous posts, should become the center of one's day and, ultimately, one's life; for, it is the "source and summit" of our lives as Christians (one must be aware of being in a state of sanctifying grace so as not to receive Our Lord unworthily); (4) renewing, each morning, one's act of total consecration, and the making of a "Morning Offering" each day (the Apostles of Light of the Immaculate Heart Marian Consecration Prayer combines one's consecration to

Our Lady with a total offering of the day's prayers, works, joys and sufferings); (5) reception of the Sacrament of Penance at least monthly; (6) performance of the five first Saturday devotion, given to Sr. Lucy at Fatima, as an act of reparation for the sins committed against to the Immaculate Heart of Mary; and (7) the wearing of a blessed Miraculous Medal, preferably around the neck.

One all-encompassing Marian Devotion

Most Catholics familiar with some or all of these Marian devotions are under the false impression that these devotions are mutually exclusive, and that it is sufficient simply to choose one from among the many and varied Marian devotions; that is, if they happen to have any Marian devotion whatsoever. The truth is that each of these devotions are sub-devotions (with, of course, the exception of the Holy Sacrifice of the Mass, which is the greatest of all prayers, and the Sacrament of Penance; for any one of the Seven Sacraments of the Church far surpasses any "devotion" whatsoever) that fall under the all-encompassing devotion of Marian Consecration. One who is truly committed to Our Lady will endeavor to practice each of these devotions, for, each of them plays an essential role in the over-arching devotion of a lived-out total consecration to the Mother of God.

St. Joseph's Espousal of the Immaculate Heart of Mary Epitomizes Total Consecration to Her

As we have seen, Marian consecration is the quickest,

easiest, perfect and most secure way of giving ourselves over to Jesus, who came to us through Mary. We must surely return to Christ using the same pathway He used in coming to us – Mary. Few will dispute the profound efficacy of Marian consecration in making strides in the spiritual life and most perfectly conforming ourselves to Christ through Mary.

There is, however, an essential aspect of this devotion that has been somewhat neglected, and that would be the role of St. Joseph. St. Joseph is numbered among the greatest of the great saints precisely because of the intimacy of life that he shared with Jesus and Mary. Moreover, we can set Joseph up as the perfect example of one who is totally consecrated to Jesus through Mary, and this due to his spousal union with the Blessed Mother. Joseph, in his espousal of Mary, gave his heart to her and took her heart as his own. There was, then, an exchange or union of hearts. And is this not precisely what takes place through consecration to Mary? For when we make a solemn act of consecration to Mary, we are, in imitation of Joseph, taking Mary's Heart and giving to her our own hearts with the goal of becoming wholly united with her, in order to love the Eucharistic Heart of Jesus with the pure, perfect and immaculate love of Mary's Immaculate Heart. Thus, Joseph was the first to consecrate himself to the Immaculate Heart of Mary, and through Mary, he was capable of loving Jesus with Mary's perfect and immaculate love. It is precisely this, then, that made St. Joseph such a great saint, and led to him becoming the Patron of the universal Church. Let us, then, follow Joseph's example by becoming one with the Immaculate Heart of Mary, in order to most perfectly unite ourselves to the Sacred Heart of Jesus. Furthermore, let us take Joseph as the patron of our total consecration to Jesus through Mary, and ask him to be the protector of Jesus and Mary in our souls.

CHAPTER FIVE

MARY,
MEDIATRIX OF ALL GRACE

Mary's indisputable role as the Mediatrix, or distributer, of every grace that springs forth from the bosom of God the Father, and that has been freely merited through the Incarnation and Redemption of Jesus Christ, her Divine Son, is even more than just a firmly established doctrine of the Ordinary Magisterium of the Church's Sacred Deposit of Faith; rather, due to the constant, unchanging and repetitive nature or essence of this particular teaching, it possesses the very nature and essence of a dogma of the faith that has yet to be declared as such. Fr. Alessandro Apollonio, F.I., has done us a tremendous service in assembling the numerous salient statements of myriad Holy Roman Pontiffs and Councils of the Church on this matter, in his marvelous article, "Mary Mediatrix of all Graces in the Pontifical Magisterium:

From Benedict XIV to Benedict XVI". For the convenience of my readers, the article has been reproduced here, below, with permission.

Why spend so much time attempting to, as it were, "prove" Our Lady's role as Mediatrix of every Grace that comes to us from God? Because it is nothing less than the absolutely firm theological foundation for that most salutary of all devotions, of which St. Louis Marie Grignion De Montfort, St. Maximilian Mary Kolbe and Pope St. John Paul II were all such staunch supporters and promulgators. If Christ Jesus is the Head of the Church, and we, His members, are the Body, then Mary is, necessarily, the "neck." Thus, everything that the Body receives from the Head travels by way of Mary; likewise, everything that the Head receives from the Body additionally travels by way of Mary. Is it any wonder, then, that Our Lady specifically asked that the Medal of the Immaculate Conception – later known as the Miraculous Medal – be worn "around the neck?"

Mary Mediatrix of all Graces in the Pontifical Magisterium: From Benedict XIV to Benedict XVI

By Fr. Alessandro M. Apollonio, F.I.
February 11, 2012
Feast of Our Lady of Lourdes
Mary, Mediatrix of All Graces, Part II

Mary's universal mediation has been the object of the

unchanging ordinary Papal Magisterium for at least the past three centuries and therefore must be considered Catholic doctrine, *definitive tenenda*, not dogmatically defined, but certainly definable (57). Despite this fact, a certain debate exists among some Mariologists today concerning the legitimacy and significance of the title *Mediatrix of all graces*. Those who deny its legitimacy generally also deny Mary's coredemption, thus witnessing the logical nexus linking these two truths (58).

Pope Benedict XIV (+1758) describes Our Blessed Lady as the "heavenly stream which brings to the hearts of wretched mortals all God's gifts and graces" (59).

Pope Pius VII (+1823) calls Mary the "Dispensatrix of all graces (*gratiarum omnium dispensatricem*)" (60).

Bl. Pius IX (+1878) places his hopes in the Most Blessed Virgin Mary, she who "with her only-begotten Son, is the most powerful Mediatrix and Conciliatrix in the whole world. ... (She) who has destroyed all heresies and snatched the faithful people and nations from all kinds of direst calamities; in her do we hope who has delivered us from so many threatening dangers" (61).

Leo XIII (+1903) writes that "with equal truth may it be also affirmed that, by the will of God, Mary is the intermediary through whom is distributed unto us this immense treasure of mercies gathered by God, for mercy and truth were created by Jesus Christ. Thus as no man goes to the Father but by the Son, so no man goes to Christ but by his Mother" (62).

In another encyclical, Leo XIII explains that in the vocal recitation of the Rosary we address first the *Father who is in heaven* and then the Virgin Mary. "Thus is confirmed that law of merciful meditation of which we have spoken, and which St. Bernardine of Siena thus expresses: 'Every grace granted to man has three degrees in order; for by God it is communicated to Christ, from Christ it passes to the Virgin, and from the Virgin it descends to us'" (63). At the end of the encyclical the Holy Father, citing the authority of St. Bernard of Clairvaux, reaffirms that God has given us a "Mediatrix" in Mary, willing "that all good should come to us by the hands of Mary" (64).

In Leo's Encyclical *Adiutricem populi*, we read that the Blessed Virgin Mary, "who was so intimately associated with the mystery of human salvation is just as closely associated with the distribution of the graces which for all time will flow from the redemption. … Among her many other titles we find her hailed as 'Our Lady, our Mediatrix,' 'the Reparatrix of the whole world,' 'the Dispenser of all heavenly gifts'" (65).

And in his Encyclical *Fidentem piumque* we read:

Undoubtedly the name and attributes of the absolute Mediator belong to no other than to Christ, for being one person, and yet both man and God, he restored the human race to the favor of the heavenly Father: *One Mediator of God and men, the man Christ Jesus, who gave himself a redemption for all* (1 Tim 2:5-6). And yet, as the Angelic Doctor teaches, *there is no reason why certain others should not be called in a certain way mediators between God and man, that is to say, in so far as they co-operate by predisposing and ministering in the union of man with God* (*Summa*, p. 3, q. 26., a. 1, 2). Such are the angels and saints, the prophets and priests of both Testaments; but especially has the Blessed Virgin a claim to the glory of this title. For no single individual can even be imagined who has ever contributed or ever will contribute so much towards reconciling man with God. She offered to mankind, hastening to eternal ruin, a Savior, at that moment when she received the announcement of the mystery of peace brought to this earth by the angel, with that admirable act of consent *in the name of the whole human race* (*Summa.* p. 3, q. 30., a. 1). She it is *from whom is born Jesus*; she is therefore truly his mother, and for this reason a worthy and acceptable "Mediatrix to the Mediator" (66).

St. Pius X (+1914), in the Encyclical *Ad diem illum*, writes:

It cannot, of course, be denied that the dispensation of these treasures is the particular and peculiar right of Jesus Christ, for they are the exclusive fruit of his death, who by his nature is the mediator between God and man. Nevertheless, by this companionship in sorrow and suffering already mentioned between the Mother and the Son, it has been allowed to the august Virgin to be the most powerful Mediatrix and Advocate of the whole world with her divine Son (*totius terrarium orbis potentissima apud unigenitum Filium suum mediatrix et conciliatrix*). The source, then, is Jesus Christ. ... But Mary ... is the channel, or, if you will, the connecting portion the function of which is to join the body to the head and to transmit to the body the influences and volitions of the head—we mean the neck. ... We are then, it will be seen, very far from attributing to the Mother of God a productive power of grace—a power which belongs to God alone. Yet, since Mary carries it over all in holiness and union with Jesus Christ, and has been associated by Jesus Christ in the work of redemption ... she is the supreme minister of the distribution of graces (*princeps largiendarum gratiarum ministra*) (67).

Pope Benedict XV (+1922), in the Apostolic Letter *Inter sodalicia* (March 22, 1918), affirms the role of Mary Co-redemptrix and Mediatrix at the foot of the Cross of her Son:

Mary suffered and, as it were, nearly died with her suffering Son; for the salvation of mankind she renounced her mother's rights and, as far as it depended on her, offered her Son to placate divine justice; so we may well say that she with Christ redeemed mankind. Consequently ... the graces which we receive from the treasury of the redemption are distributed, so to speak, by the hands of this sorrowful Virgin (68).

In the context of the canonization of St. Joan of Arc, Benedict XV observed that "every grace and blessing comes to us" by means of Our Blessed Lady. Therefore, besides the intercession of the saints, "one must include the influence of her whom the Holy Fathers greeted with the title, *Mediatrix omnium gratiam*" (69).

On January 12, 1921, the Holy See received the requests of Cardinal Mercier (archbishop primate of Belgium) and of the Belgian bishops, approving the Mass and Office of the Feast of the *Blessed Virgin Mary Mediatrix of all graces*, established on the date of May 31. The liturgical celebration of this feast was granted to the dioceses of Belgium and to all dioceses and religious orders requesting it (70).

With the Apostolic Letter *Sodalitatem Nostrae Dominae*, Benedict XV granted plenary and partial indulgences to the *Sodalizio di Nostra Signora della buona morte* (Association of Our Lady of a Happy Death); he also granted indulgences for the day of May 31, Feast of the Blessed Virgin Mary "Mediatrix of all graces" (71).

Pius XI (+1939) calls the Virgin Mary the "Mediatrix of all graces with God" (72); he writes that Christ has associated Mary with himself as "minister and mediatress of grace" (73); he makes reference to the most efficacious patronage of the Blessed Virgin Mary "Mediatrix of all graces" (74); he establishes the Blessed Virgin Mary of graces of Mount Philerimos as the principal patroness of the Archdiocese of Rhodes; and, in the related document, the Blessed Virgin is called "Mediatrix of all graces" (75).

Pius XII (+1958) very often makes use of the titles *Mediatrix omnium gratiarum, gratiarum omnium apud Deum sequestra,* and other similar expressions (76). In the Encyclical *Ad Caeli Reginam,* Pius XII wonderfully illustrates the doctrine of the Blessed Virgin Mary's universal mediation:

Certainly, in the full and strict meaning of the term, only Jesus Christ, the God-man, is King; but Mary, too, as Mother of the divine Christ, as his associate in the redemption, in his struggle with his enemies and his final victory over them, has a share, though in a limited and analogous way, in his royal dignity. For from her union with Christ she attains a radiant eminence transcending that of any other creature; from her union with Christ she receives the royal right to dispose of the treasures of the divine Redeemer's kingdom; from her union with Christ finally comes the inexhaustible efficacy of her maternal intercession before the Son and his Father. Hence it cannot be doubted that Mary most holy is far above all other creatures in dignity, and after her Son possesses primacy over all. ...

For if through his humanity the divine Word performs miracles and gives graces, if he uses his sacraments and saints as instruments for the salvation of men, why should he not make use of the role and work of his most holy Mother in imparting to us the fruits of redemption? "With a heart that is truly a mother's," to quote again our predecessor of immortal memory, Pius IX, "does she approach the problem of our salvation, and is solicitous for the whole human race; made Queen of heaven and earth by the Lord, exalted above all choirs of angels and saints, and standing at the right hand of her only Son,

Jesus Christ our Lord, she intercedes powerfully for us with a mother's prayers, obtains what she seeks, and cannot be refused." On this point another of our predecessors of happy memory, Leo XIII, has said that an "almost immeasurable" power has been given Mary in the distribution of graces; St. Pius X adds that she fills this office "as by the right of a mother" (77).

Bl. John XXIII (+1962) granted the title and privilege of minor basilica to the church dedicated to the Blessed Virgin Mary Mediatrix of All Graces, Sultana of Africa, located in the locality of Lodonga, in Uganda. In the text of the related apostolic letter there are three references to the "Mediatrix of all graces" (78).

The Mediation of the Blessed Virgin Mary at the Second Vatican Council

On November 21, 1964, after an editorial work of about four years (if we include the preparatory work before the Council), Paul VI promulgated the Dogmatic Constitution *Lumen Gentium*, the eighth chapter of which is entirely dedicated to the Mother of God and of men (79). Before arriving at this definitive text, there was no shortage of lively discussions on the title of Mediatrix. Many bishops asked for its dogmatic definition, but others were opposed to it for various reasons, not the least of which were those of an ecumenical nature (80).

Among the Fathers of the Central Preparatory Commission of the Second Vatican Council, 16 expressed reservation with the Marian title of *Mediatrix* (81). The use of the title would damage the ecumenical dialogue with the Protestants (82). Archbishop Alter (Cincinnati, Ohio), with cardinals Koenig (Vienna, Austria) and Godfrey (Westminster), echoed these sentiments (83). Instead of *mediation*, Cardinal Montini preferred to speak of the Blessed Virgin's spiritual maternity, her regality and her intercession (84).

Fr. Paolo Siano rightly observes in his above-cited article that there was, in this attitude, a kind of opposition to the pontifical thought, because, almost on the morrow of the conclusion of these discussions, July 23, 1962, Bl. John XXIII approved the new Missal which contained the Holy Mass to the *Beata Maria Virgo omnium gratiarum Mediatrix* (*Blessed Virgin Mary, Mediatrix of all graces*) (85).

During the Second Vatican Council, particularly in the third session held in 1964, there was a lively discussion on various Mariological themes, and there was also a discussion on the title of Mediatrix (86). Such a title was commonly accepted by everyone, but a few, including cardinals Alfrink, Léger and Bea, who preferred it to be omitted from the official documents of the Council in order to promote ecumenism toward Protestant Christians (the great majority of whom rejected the title then and continue to reject it presently) (87). There were, in fact, rumors that the Protestants were threatening to break off all ecumenical dialogue if the title of Mediatrix were to be inserted into the conciliar dogmatic constitution. Meanwhile, 310 Council Fathers desired an authoritative, extraordinary and dogmatic pronouncement by the Council in favor of Mary's mediation-coredemption (88). To reconcile the two parties it was decided to insert the title of Mediatrix into the Marian document of the Council, but also to include adequate explanations to respond to Protestant objections and to omit all examination regarding the nature of this mediation.

The Protestant "observers" invited to the Council were not satisfied, but they did not break off the dialogue (89). The omission of the title, in fact, would have cast a shadow upon the preceding Ordinary Magisterium and could have perhaps diverted the ecumenical dialogue from the level of truth to the level of political ambiguity. It could have contributed to "maintaining rather than dissipating the ambiguous" at the service of a "mistaken ecumenism" (90).

Fr. Carlo Balić (O.F.M., +1977), one of the original drafters of chapter 8 of *Lumen Gentium*, provides a suitable response to those who wish to interpret the Council as the moment of departure from the preceding Mariological tradition: "The Council has not mitigated or deprived the concept of the mediation of the Virgin of its content in the sense in which in which it has been propagated by the theologians of our (twentieth) century" (91).

In examining the conciliar text of No. 62 of *Lumen Gentium*, we read the following:

Taken up to heaven she did not lay aside this salvific duty, but by her constant intercession continued to bring us the gifts of eternal salvation. By her maternal charity, she cares for the brethren of her Son, who still journey on earth surrounded by dangers and difficulties, until they are led into the happiness of their true home. Therefore the Blessed Virgin is invoked by the Church under the titles of Advocate, Auxiliatrix, Adjutrix, and Mediatrix. This, however, is to be so understood that it neither takes away from nor adds anything to the dignity and efficaciousness of Christ the one Mediator (92).

That is why, in the Church, the Blessed Virgin Mary is also invoked under the title of "Mediatrix." The Council document cites other magisterial documents as proof of the complete catholicity of the title: Leo XIII, *Adiutricem populi*; St. Pius X, *Ad diem illum*; Pius XI, *Miserentissimus Redemptor*; Pius XII, *Nuntius Radiophonicus* (in *AAS* 38 (1946) 266).

In order to prevent an interpretation of Marian mediation as "mere" intercession, many Council Fathers proposed the Marian title of "Dispensatrix of all graces," already fully accepted by the Magisterium and perfectly in conformity to common Catholic doctrine. The Doctrinal Commission replied that the Council text did not intend to deny this doctrine (93). Therefore, the Second Vatican Council does not at all repudiate the doctrine of *Mary Mediatrix of all graces* (94), a doctrine also clearly taught in the papal documents expressly cited by the Council text.

Paul VI (+1978): He preferred to speak of Mary as our intercessor (95) with Christ rather than as Dispensatrix of graces (96), but this is a question of a different emphasis, not of a denial. Still, Pope Paul VI was certainly less inclined to speak on these subjects than his predecessors, from Leo XIII to Pius XII.

By a faculty granted by Paul VI, Cardinal James Lercaro, assisted by the Secretary Msgr. Annibale Bugnini, approved and confirmed the "Proper" of the Masses of the Order of Friars Minor Capuchin, for use in the Italian provinces (97), in which is found the Mass of "Mary Most Holy Mediatrix of All Grace," a feast of third class, on the date of May 8 (98).
In the Apostolic Exhortation *Signum Magnum*, Paul VI recalls that Mary, assumed into heaven, assists her still-pilgrim children:

> She makes herself their Advocate, Auxiliatrix, Adjutrix and Mediatrix. Of this intercession of hers for the People of God with the Son, the Church has been persuaded, ever since the first centuries, as testified to by this most ancient antiphon which, with some slight difference, forms part of the liturgical prayer in the East as well as in the West: "We seek refuge under the protection of your mercies, Oh Mother of God; do not reject our supplication in need but save us from perdition, O you who alone are blessed." ... Therefore, as each one of us can repeat with St. Paul: "The Son of God loved me and gave himself up for me," (Gal 2:29) so in all trust he

can believe that the divine Savior has left to him also, in spiritual heritage, his Mother, with all the treasures of grace and virtues with which he had endowed her, that she may pour them over us through the influence of her powerful intercession and our willing imitation. This is why St. Bernard rightly affirms: "Coming to her the Holy Spirit filled her with grace for herself; when the same Spirit pervaded her again she became superabundant and redounding in grace for us also" (99).

At the end of the apostolic exhortation the Pope remembers the 25th anniversary of the "consecration" of the Church and of the human race to the Immaculate Heart of Mary and exhorts "all the sons of the Church to renew personally their consecration to the Immaculate Heart of the Mother of the Church" (100).

In his letter to Cardinal Suenens, archbishop of Malines-Brussels, on the occasion of the Marian International Congress of May 13, 1975, Paul VI writes:

> In confirmation of these reflections, we are happy to recall the testimony that also the Fathers and Doctors of the Eastern church, exemplary as they are in the faith and in worship of the Holy Spirit, have borne to ecclesial faith and the cult of the Mother of Christ, as the mediator of divine favors. Their affirmations, however surprising, should not disturb anyone, since it is understood and sometimes clearly

mentioned in them that the source of the Virgin's mediating action is dependent on the action of the Spirit of God. So, for example, St. Ephraem exalts Mary in these superlative tones: "Blessed is she who has been made the source for the whole world, emanating all goods" (S. Ephraem Syri hymni et serm., ed. Th. Lamy Malines, 1882-1902, II, p. 548); and again: "Most holy Lady … the only one that has been made the dwelling of all the graces of the Holy Spirit" (Assem. græc. III, 542). St. John Chrysostom sums up Mary's salvific work in the following stupendous eulogy: "A virgin chased us out of paradise; thanks to the intervention of another virgin, we have found eternal life again. As we were condemned by the fault of a virgin, so we have been crowned by the merit of a virgin" (Expos. in ps. 44, 7: PG 55, 193). They are echoed, in the eighth century, by St. Germanus of Constantinople, who addresses the following moving invocations to Mary: "You, oh pure, excellent and most merciful Lady, comfort of Christians, … protect us with the wings of your kindness; guard us with your intercession, giving us eternal life; you who are the hope of Christians that does not deceive. … Your gifts are innumerable. For no one, unless through you, oh holy one, obtains salvation. No one, unless through you, is delivered from evil. Who like you, in agreement with your only Son, looks after mankind?" (*Concio in sanctam Mariam*: PG 98, 327).

This traditional faith, which is common both to the

Eastern and to the Western Church, found authoritative confirmation in the teaching of our great predecessor Leo XIII, who, while he published numerous encyclical letters to promote the cult of the Mother of God, invoked especially under the title of Queen of the Holy Rosary, also dedicated a long document encyclical to the exaltation, even more excellent, of the Holy Spirit and promotion of his worship (Enc. Divinum illud munus, May 9, 1897; Acta Leonis, Vol. XVII, pp. 126-128) (101).

John Paul II (+2005) brought the title of *Mary Mediatrix of all graces* back into favor, despite the reticence of a few theologians who appealed to a restrictive interpretation of conciliar Mariology (102). Pope John Paul II used the title "Mediatrix of all graces" literally at least seven times in his addresses (homilies, discourses, angelus, etc.) (103), according to the research conducted by Msgr. Arthur Burton Calkins, Dr. Mark Miravalle, Don Manfred Hauke (104), and Fr. Paolo Siano, F.I. (105)

On other occasions John Paul II used the expressions "Universal Mediatrix of all grace" (106), "Mother of all graces" (107), "Dispensatrix of all grace" (108), giver of "all grace" (109), "Mediatrix of all grace" (110), and "Mediatrix of graces" (111).

In the Marian Encyclical *Redemptoris Mater* (March 25, 1989), the Pontiff of *Totus Tuus* illustrates in an in-depth manner the theology of Mary's *maternal mediation*.
In the "Parish Priest's Prayer to Mary Most Holy" contained in the appendix to the Instruction of the

Congregation for the Clergy, *The Priest, Pastor and Leader of the Parish Community* (August 4, 2002), Our Blessed Lady is also invoked with the title "Mediatrix of all graces" (112).

Contained in the *Collectio missarum de beata Virgine*, approved and promulgated by John Paul II on the occasion of the Marian Year (113) is a Mass of the *Virgin Mary Mother and Mediatrix of grace*; in the preface of this Mass, we read that the Most Blessed Virgin Mary carries out "a maternal role in the Church: of intercession, of pardon, of prayer and grace, of reconciliation and peace" (114). The Virgin Mary is "Mother of mercy and handmaid of grace" (115). The title of *Dispensatrix of grace* reappears in other eucological texts of the same *Collectio Missarum* (116).

As proof that the title of *Mediatrix*, in the broadest sense, includes that of *Co-Redemptrix*, John Paul II did not hesitate to use the former as well as the latter term. In his article cited above, Fr. Siano has identified a seventh Woytylian text in which the title of *Co-Redemptrix* appears (117), complementing the other six references previously "discovered" by Msgr. Calkins.

Pope Benedict XVI has recently continued the overall succession of papal writers on Our Lady's role as Mediatrix of all graces. In his May 11, 2007, homily in which he canonized the Brazilian Franciscan, Fr. Antônio de Sant'ana Galvão, O.F.M., Benedict XVI uses the extraordinary foundation of the Marian mediation of every grace of the redemption in a generous manner somewhat reminiscent of St.

Bernard, St. Louis-Marie and St. Maximilian: "There is no fruit of grace in the history of salvation that does not have as its necessary instrument the mediation of Our Lady" (118).

Benedict reiterates the essence of Marian mediation as he continues: "Let us give thanks to God the Father, to God the Son, to God the Holy Spirit from whom, through the intercession of the Virgin Mary, we receive all the blessings of heaven" (119).

The Nature of the Blessed Virgin Mary's Influence in the Application of the Redemption

The fact of this mystery of the maternal mediation of Mary here and now, both as intercession and as spiritual begetting of Christ within the minds and hearts of all believers, since the golden age of scholastic theology (thirteenth century), has led to a great deal of speculation on the nature of this mediation and the type of causal influence exercised directly and immediately by a human person on the souls of other men, such as in fact is ascribed to the Virgin Mother as Mediatrix of all graces. Neither the terminology employed by the representatives of various schools of theology, such as the Thomistic and Scotistic, even within the same school is uniform, nor are the concepts behind the terminology uniformly defined. Hence for those not fully informed about these discussions the significance of the speculation is hard to grasp. Nor is it necessary for all to grasp it in order to appreciate the meaning and importance of the maternal mediation of Mary here and now.

Briefly, those who follow a Thomistic orientation tend to stress the importance of what is called "physical-instrumental" causality to appreciate in some way the mystery of this mediation and its relevance to many practical, spiritual, pastoral, missionary dimensions of Christian life. Those of the Scotistic persuasion tend to stress more the moral, exemplary, meritorious aspects of causal activity to illustrate not merely the intercession (advocacy) of Mary at the throne of grace in heaven where she is gloriously assumed, but also the unique personal, or voluntary, features of her direct action in the Church and on souls for the distribution of all graces. Without doubt valid points are made by both approaches, and neither exhausts the subject, nor can pretend to do so (120).

With Pope John Paul II, however, a certain impulse was given to reopening these speculative discussions, not only on the very nature of mediation in Christ and Mary as a unique form of causality (on which rests that of the sacramental order), but also of others, not much discussed in the speculative realm since the middle ages. I refer here to the role of Mary as Mediatrix in the sacramental order and the manner in which she directly and immediately touches the heart of every one of her spiritual children (121). Both Pope John Paul II and his successor, Benedict XVI, have spoken of the Marian principle of the Church and the unique place of Mary at the very heart of the Church (122). This is simply another way of talking about Marian mediation, but it is also a way of setting study of grace and free will, and still more the indwelling of the Holy Spirit in the Church and in every believer in the state of grace, in a radically Marian context. St. Maximilian M. Kolbe does more than hint at all this in speaking of transubstantiation into the Immaculate, as she is transubstantiated into the Holy Spirit, in order to "mediate" in the order of conversion and sanctification (123).

That these discussions should continue is not something otiose. Not only do the metaphysical insights of Christian philosophers help us to enter more profoundly into the understanding of an extremely important feature of our faith, one in the thirteenth century described as the very foundation and primary character of the spirituality of St. Francis of Assisi (124), and repeated again in our times by St. Maximilian M. Kolbe, this time however in reference to the spiritual and intellectual life of the Church: Mary, mother and teacher (125), but the very effort to undertake such speculations bears fruit in the form of a deepened appreciation of the basic themes of Christian philosophy. A medieval English Benedictine Abbot, Odo of Canterbury, an older contemporary of St. Francis, in a homily preached around the year 1200, called not Aristotle, but Mary our philosopher and added also our philosophy (126). For the love of wisdom cannot merely be an abstraction, but of that person who is Wisdom incarnate, the Way, the Truth and the Life, loved as only the Virgin Mother can know and love the Wisdom who became her Child.

Conclusion

With the Encyclical *Redemptoris Mater* (March 25, 1987) of John Paul II, a step forward has been taken in the theological comprehension of Mary's mediation in the light of her maternity. The excellent theological intuition of the Pope is completely summarized in the simple and effective title of Mary as *maternal Mediatrix*. What is maternity if not an excellent form of mediation from every point of view, in particular the personal and spiritual? We could define it as the feminine mode of collaborating with God in the generation of the natural and supernatural life of persons. Since it puts the woman in an intermediary position between God, source of life, and the child, who receives it, in which she unites the two extremes (God and the child) to each other, this maternal collaboration is true mediation. Evidently, understanding of the maternal mediation of Mary which touches both heaven and earth is crucial not only in the spiritual order, but wherever fundamental questions of human existence arise, whether personal or social, familial or political. Without some essential reference to the mystery of Mary, attempted resolutions of such problems can only end in human tragedy, and betrayal of our dear Savior.

But while the mother is always a mediatrix, not every mediation is maternal. Christ, in fact, is Mediator but not mother; Mary, instead, was maternal Mediatrix before being physically mother, because her mediation was completely oriented and preordained, from the moment of conception, to the divine-human maternity. When the woman collaborates with God in procreation, she is always a mother. She is a natural mother if mother of a natural life, a supernatural mother if mother of a supernatural life, divine Mother if mother of the divine Life. And supernatural maternity is true maternity not only and not so much by analogy to natural maternity, but above all by its reference to the exemplar (or *analogatum princeps*— major analogue), or to Mary's divine-human maternity, in which every maternity, natural and supernatural, finds its own incomparable perfection.

Reflection on the theological concept of mediation found in the Pauline corpus and serving as a kind of profound synthesis of all aspects of the mystery of salvation as this is grounded in the order of the hypostatic union, viz., of the joint predestination of Jesus and Mary, illumines the profound insights of the late Holy Father. In turn these enable us to see that there is nothing inherently contradictory in insisting on the unicity and sufficiency of Christ's mediation and at the same time affirming his Mother as our maternal Mediatrix. And that seen, the mystery of Marian mediation appears everywhere in Scripture and Tradition, in the liturgy and in sacred art, sometimes with, sometimes without the title. Nor will we be inclined to underestimate the importance of this mystery, practically as well as speculatively. This is but another way of saying that the presence of Mary here and now is crucial to our understanding and love of Christ, to our sharing in the fruits of redemption. Mary is our Mediatrix with Christ as Christ is our Mediator with the Father. Put in the more humble language of the street: know Mary, know Jesus; no Mary, no Jesus. That is the bottom line making the difference between heaven and hell. That is why true devotion to Jesus means total consecration to the Immaculate Mediatrix, why we can never say enough about Mary, why we can never be too devoted to Mary (127). For she is our Mother, the Immaculate Mediatrix, ever sustaining us as disciples of her Son.

Notes

(57) We will follow the outline of the positive historical study of Fr. Paolo M. Siano, F.I., which may be consulted upon further inquiries. P. Siano, F.I., *Uno studio su Maria Santissima "Mediatrice di tutte le Grazie" nel magistero pontificio fino al pontificato di Giovanni Paolo II*, op. cit.

(58) Cf. A. Apollonio, F.I., *Il "calvario teologico" della Corredenzione mariana*, Presentation of Fr. Paolo M. Siano (pp. 3-6), Casa Mariana Editrice, Castelpetroso 1999, pp. 43. Standing out, unfortunately, among the voices contrary to the Marian title of "Co-redemptrix" and "Mediatrix of all Graces" is that of Salvatore Perella, O.S.M., *Virgo Ecclesia facta. La Madre di Dio tra due millenni. Summa storico-teologica*, Miles Immaculatae, Anno XXXVII, fasc. II, 2001, pp. 357-434. See in particular pp. 408-410.

(59) Benedict XIV, Bull *Gloriosae Dominae*, 1748, *Op. Omnia*, v. 16, ed. Prati, 1846, p. 428, cit. in *Our Lady: Papal Teachings*, trans. Daughters of St. Paul (Boston: St. Paul Editions, 1961), p. 26, n. 4.

(60) Pius VII, *Ampliatio privilegiorum ecclesiae B.M. Virginis ab angelo salutatae in cenobio Fratrum Ordinis Servorum B.M.V. Florentiae, A.D.*, 1806, § 1, in J.J. Bourassé, *Summa Aurea de laudibus Beatissimae Virginis Mariae, Dei Genitricis sine labe conceptae...*, Tomus VII, Paris 1862, col. 546.

(61) Pius IX, Apostolic Constitution *Ineffabilis Deus*, December 8, 1854, in R. Spiazzi, O.P., ed., *Maria Santissima nel Magistero della Chiesa. I documenti pontifici da Pio IX a Giovanni Paolo II*, Massimo, Milano 1987, p. 38.

(62) Leo XIII, Encyclical on the Rosary *Octobri mense*, September 21, 1891, in H. Denzinger, *Enchiridion symbolorum definitionum et declarationum de rebus fidei et morum, bilingual edizione*, ed. Peter

Hünermann, EDB, Bologna 1996, n. 3274. Abbreviation: Denz. The entire text of the encyclical is in *Acta Sanctae Sedis (ASS)*, 24 (1891-1892) 193-203.

(63) Leo XIII, Encyclical on the Rosary *Iucunda semper*, September 8, 1894, in *ASS* 27 (1894-1895) 179.

(64) Cf. *ibid.*, pp. 183-184.

(65) Leo XIII, Encyclical *Adiutricem populi*, September 5, 1895, in *ASS* 28 (1895-1896) 130-131. in R. Spiazzi, ed., *Maria Santissima nel Magistero della Chiesa. I documenti pontifici da Pio IX a Giovanni Paolo II*, Massimo, Milano 1987, p. 60 (*ASS* 28 (1895-1896) 130-131).

(66) Leo XIII, Encyclical *Fidentem piumque*, September 20, 1896, in *ASS* 29 (1896-1897) 206 (Denz. 3320-3321).

(67) Pius X, Encyclical *Ad diem illum*, February 2, 1904, in *ASS* 36 (1903-1904) 449-462.

(68) Benedict XV, Apostolic Letter *Inter sodalicia*, March 22, 1918, in R. Spiazzi, op. cit., p. 87 (Denz. 3370). English translation cit. in *Papal Teachings: Our Lady*, op. cit., p. 194, nn. 267-268.

(69) Benedict XV, Decree of April 6, 1919, cited by Hauke M., *Maria "Mediatrice di tutte le grazie." La mediazione universale di Maria nell'opera teologica e pastorale di cardinale Mercier*, art. cit., p. 64. English translation cit. by M. Hauke, *Mary, Mediatress of Grace: Mary's Mediation of Grace in the Theological and Pastoral Works of Cardinal Mercier*, Supplement to *Mary at the Foot of the Cross IV*, op. cit., p. 52.

(70) Cf. *ibid.*, pp. 67-72.

(71) Benedict XV, Apostolic Letter *Sodalitatem Nostrae Dominae*, May 31, 1921, *Acta Apostolicae Sedis (AAS)* 13 (1921) 345.

(72) Pius XI, Apostolic Letter *Galliam, Ecclesiae filiam*, March 2, 1922, *AAS* 14 (1922) 186.

(73) Pius XI, Encyclical *Miserentissimus Redemptor*, May 8, 1928, *AAS* 20 (1928) 178.

(74) Pius XI, Encyclical *Caritate Christi compulsi*, May 3, 1932, in *AAS* 24 (1932) 192.

(75) Pius XI, Apostolic Letter *Rhodiensis archidioecesis*, October 4, 1934, in *AAS* 26 (1934) 545-546.

(76) Pius XII, Apostolic Letter *Claverenses dioecesis*, August 5, 1942, in *AAS* 34 (1942) 364; idem, Apostolic Letter *Beatissimae Virgini*, August 15, 1942, in *AAS* 34 (1942) 365; idem, radio message *Benedicite Deum caeli*, October 31, 1942, AAS 34 (1942) 317; idem, radio message *Bendito seja o Senor*, May 13, 1946, AAS

38 (1946) 264; idem, Apostolic Letter *Hungaricae gentis*, March 25, 1948, *AAS* 40 (1948) 499; Id., Apostolic Letter *Maximo Nos*, October 10, 1949, AAS 44 (1952) 808; idem, Apostolic Letter *Imaginem Beatae*, July 31, 1950, *AAS* 43 (1951) 111; idem, Apostolic Letter *Caelorum Reginae*, July 31, 1950, *AAS* 43 (1951) 79; idem, Apostolic Letter *Mirum sane*, July 31, 1950, *AAS* 43 (1951) 156; idem, radio message *Quando lasciate*, December 8, 1953, *AAS* 45 (1953) 849-850; idem, Apostolic Letter *Eadem ratione*, June 30, 1954, *AAS* 47 (1955) 710; idem, radio message *On the occasion of the fourth centenary of the foundation of the city of Sao Paolo, Brazil*, September 7, 1954, AAS 46 (1954) 546; idem, Apostolic Constitution *Sedes sapientiae*, May 31, 1956, AAS 48 (1956) 354, in D. Bertetto, ed., *Il Magistero mariano di Pio XII. Edizione italiana di tutti i documenti mariani di Pio XII*, (Rome: Edizioni Paoline, 1960), p. 641; idem, Apostolic Letter *In vitae huius*, January 4, 1958, in AAS 51 (1959) 159.

The Latin feminine noun, *sequestra, -ae*, is equivalent to *mediatrix*. Cf. L. Castiglioni – S. Mariotti, *Vocabolario della lingua latina. Latino-Italiano, Italiano-Latino*, (Rome: Loescher Editore, 1990), p. 1040.

(77) Pius XII, Encyclical *Ad Caeli Reginam*, October 11, 1954, in AAS 46 (1954) 635-637.

(78) Cf. John XXIII, Apostolic Letter *Beatissimam Virginem Mariam*, May 26, 1961, in AAS 65 (1961) 150-151.

(79) Cf. G. Besutti, O.S.M., *Lo schema mariano al Concilio Vaticano II. Documentazione e note di cronaca*, (Rome: Edition Marianum— Libreria Desclée, 1966), pp. 183-185.

(80) For the story of Chapter 8 of *Lumen Gentium*, see E. Toniolo, O.S.M., *La beata Vergine nel Concilio Vaticano II, Centro di Cultura Mariana "Madre della Chiesa,"* Rome 2004, 453 pp.

(81) Cf. G. Besutti, *Lo schema mariano del Concilio Vaticano II*, op. cit., p. 22. Among this group was the Archbishop of Milan, Cardinal John Baptist Montini, who declared "inopportune, indeed, harmful" the presentation of the title of Mediatrix, since—as the illustrious cardinal explained—in the first place, "the term Mediator must be attributed solely and exclusively to Christ" according to St. Paul's teaching (cf. 1 Tim 2:5).

(82) Cf. Acta et Documenta Concilio Oecumenico Vaticano II apparando, Series II (Preparatoria), Volumen II: Acta pontificiae Commissionis Centralis praeparatoriae Concilii Oecumenici

JAYSON M. BRUNELLE, M.Ed., CAGS

Vaticani, Pars IV: Sessio septima, 12-19 Iunii 1962, Vatican City 1968, p. 777, cited by A. Escudero Cabello, *La cuestión de la mediación mariana en la preparación del Vaticano II*, Libreria Ateneo Salesiano, Rome 1997, pp. 251-253.

(83) Cf. A. Escudero Cabello, op. cit., p. 251.

(84) Acta et Documenta Concilio Oecumenico Vaticano II apparando, Series II (Preparatoria), Volumen II: Acta pontificiae Commissionis Centralis praeparatoriae Concilii Oecumenici Vaticani, Pars IV: Sessio septima, 12-19 Iunii 1962, Vatican City 1968, p. 777, cited by A. Escudero Cabello, *op. cit.*, p. 260.

(85) Proprium Sanctorum pro aliquibus locis, 8 maii Beatae Mariae Virginis omnium gratiarum Mediatricis, in Missale Romanum ex decreto SS. Concilii Tridentini restitutum Summorum Pontificum cura recognitum, editio typica, Typis Plyglottis Vaticanis 1962, pp. (159)-(160).

(86) Cf. G. Besutti, *Lo schema mariano del Concilio Vaticano II. Documentazione e note di cronaca*, Rome: Marianum-Desclée, 1966; G. Roschini, O.S.M., *Maria santissima nella storia della salvezza*, vol. II, (Isola del Liri: Pisani, 1969), pp. 111-116; idem, *La Mediazione mariana oggi*, (Rome: Pontificia Facoltà Teologica "Marianum" – Istituto di Mariologia, Edizioni "Marianum," 1971), pp. 47-49; A. Escudero Cabello, S.D.B., La cuestión de la mediación en la preparación del Vaticano II, LAS, Rome, 1997; E. Toniolo, O.S.M., *La beata Maria Vergine nel Concilio Vaticano II*, Centro di cultura mariana "Madre della Chiesa," Rome, 2004, 453 pp.

(87) For a Protestant defense of Mediatrix, cf. J. Macquarrie, "Mary Co-redemptrix and Disputes over Justification and Grace: An Anglican View," *Mary Co-redemptrix. Doctrinal Issues Today*, pp. 139-150, and C. Dickson, *"Mary Mediatrix: A Protestant Response," Mary Coredemptrix, Mediatrix, Advocate: Theological foundations III. Contemporary Insights on a Fifth Marian Dogma*, pp. 181-184.

(88) This is the number that results from the examination of the written requests preserved in the Council archive. Obviously an even greater number must be presumed, because, while everyone who submitted the written requests were in favor, not everyone who was in favor submitted a written request, as is always the case with contingent matters. Cf. A. Escudero Cabello, *La cuestion de la mediación mariana...*, op. cit., p. 88. According to Fr. Roschini, the written requests numbered about 400 (cf. Roschini G., *La Mediazione mariana oggi*, Pontificia Facoltà Teologica "Marianum" – Istituto di Mariologia, Edizioni "Marianum,"

72

Rome 1971, p. 47).

(89) They could not reasonably justify the imposition of their Protestant beliefs upon an essentially Catholic ecumenical council.

(90) C. Journet, *De la Vierge Marie et la Collegialité*, in *Nova et vetera*, 2 (1965) 109.

(91) C. Balić, O.F.M., *El Capitulo VIII de la Constitución "Lumen Gentium" Comparado con el Primer Esquema de la Beata Virgen Madre de la Iglesia, Estudios Marianos*, 27 (1966) 169.

(92) Vatican II Council, Costituzione dogmatica *Lumen gentium*, November 21, 1964, n. 62.

(93) Cf. Roschini G., *Maria Santissima nella storia della salvezza*, vol. II, op. cit., p. 202.

(94) Besides the Protestants and Jansenists, included among those who deny this doctrine are a few modern ecumenists and all modernist ecumenists. Critical opposition is widespread: even some of the writings of Abbot Laurentin are infected by this criticism (cf. R. Laurentin, *La Vergine Maria. Mariologia postconciliare*, Rome: Edizione Paoline, 1973, pp. 302-304).

(95) Cf. Paul VI, Letter for the 750th Anniversary of the Indulgence of the Portiuncula, July 14, 1966, in *Encicliche e discorsi di S.S. Paolo VI*, vol. X, May-August 1966, (Rome: Edizioni Paoline, 1967), p. 256; *idem*, address to a group of Hungarian pilgrims, in *Encicliche e discorsi di S.S. Paolo VI*, vol. XXIII, January-December 1972, (Rome: Edizioni Paoline, 1973), p. 299; *idem*, Apostolic Letter *Le Memorie apostoliche*, May 2, 1974, in *Insegnamenti di Paolo VI*, vol. XII, 1974, p. 500; idem, general audience, May 14, 1975, in *Insegnamenti di Paolo VI*, vol. XIII, 1975, p. 502; idem allocution to the participants of the International Marian-Mariological Congress, May 16, 1975, in *Insegnamenti di Paolo VI*, vol. XIII, 1975, p. 522; idem, address to German-speaking pilgrims, August 15, 1975, in *Insegnamenti di Paolo VI*, vol. XIII, 1975, p. 854.

(96) Cf. Paul VI, Encyclical Christi Matri, September 15, 1966, in Enchiridion Vaticanum. Omissa 1962-1987, Supplementum I, EDB, Bologna 2000, n. 94, p. 87; idem, General audience, May 30, 1974, in Insegnamenti di Paolo VI, vol. XI, 1973, (Vatican City: Tipografia Poliglotta Vaticana, 1974), p. 475.

(97) Consilium ad Exsequendam Constitutione de Sacra Liturgia, Prot. N. 3577/65, in *Proprio dei Santi dell'Ordine dei Frati Minori*

Cappuccini, (Turin-Rome: Casa Editrice Marietti—Centro Nazionale T.O.F. Cappuccini, 1966), p. (2).

(98) *Proprio dei Santi dell'Ordine dei Frati Minori Cappuccini* May 8th (Mass of) "Maria SS. Mediatrice di ogni grazia," in Messale Romano quotidiano, 1966, pp. (50)-(52).

(99) Paul VI, Apostolic Exhortation *Signum magnum*, May 13, 1967, 2.5, in *Enchiridion Vaticanum*, vol. II. 1963-1967, (Bologna, Italy: EDB, 1992), pp. 987, 999.

(100) *Ibid.*, 8, in *Enchiridion Vaticanum*, vol. II, p. 1003.

(101) Paul VI, *Lettera al Card. Leo Jozef Suenens in occasione del Congresso Mariano Internazionale – La Vergine Maria nell'opera dell'umana Redenzione*, May 13, 1975, in *Insegnamenti di Paolo VI*, vol. XIII, 1975 (Vatican City: Tipografia Poliglotta Vaticana, 1976), pp. 495-496. English cit. by P. Siano, *Mary 'Mediatrix of All Graces' in the Papal Magisterium up to the Pontificate of Paul VI*, to be published in *Mary at the Foot of the Cross VII: Coredemptrix, Therefore Mediatrix of all Graces*. See note 1.

(102) Cf. S. Perrella, *Maria Serva del Signore e della Redenzione. Tra richieste e approfondimenti*, in *Miles Immaculatae*, fasc. 2, July-December 1998, pp. 262-263; T. Sennott, "Mary Mediatrix of All Graces, Vatican Council II and Ecumenism," *Miles Immaculatae*, fasc. 1-2, 1988, pp. 151-167.

(103) John Paul II, Allocution, in *L'Osservatore Romano*, Monday-Tuesday, January 18-19, 1988, p. 1; idem, *L'Osservatore Romano*, Monday-Tuesday, April 11-12, 1988, Supplement n. 84, p. IV; *idem*, in *L'Osservatore Romano*, Monday-Tuesday, July 2-3, 1990, p. 5; *idem*, in *L'Osservatore Romano*, Saturday, June 29, 1996, p. 5; *idem*, Apostolic Letter *Amor Noster*, April 30, 1980, in AAS 72 (1980) 384-385; *idem*, Apostolic Letter *Frequentissimae dioeceses*, in *AAS* 79 (1987) 437.

(104) Cf. M. Hauke , *La Mediazione materna di Maria secondo Papa Giovanni Paolo II*, in *Aa. Vv.*, *Maria Corredentrice. Storia e Teologia. VII*, Bibliotheca Corredemptionis B.V. Mariae, Casa Mariana Editrice, Frigento 2005, pp. 86-88. Concerning these passages of Pope John Paul II (in which he makes reference to the *Mediatrix of all graces* or other similar expressions), Don Hauke makes reference to Msgr. Calkins (cf. Hauke, *op. cit.*, p. 86, note 107). On Mary "Co-redemptrix" and "Mediatrix" in the Marian Magisterium of John Paul II, see also Msgr. Calkins' recent study, A.B. Calkins, ed., *Totus Tuus. Il magistero mariano di Giovanni Paolo II*, preface by Msgr. Carlo Caffana, archbishop of Bologna,

(Siena, Italy: Edizioni Cantagalli, 2006), pp. 242-245, 306-319. (Msgr. Calkins has also recently presented the results of his study in English at the 7th Annual Symposium on Marian Coredemption: *Mary, Mediatrix of All Graces in the Papal Magisterium of Pope John Paul II*, to be published in *Mary at the Foot of the Cross VII: Coredemptrix, Therefore Mediatrix of all Graces*. See note 1.) In other pronouncements, Pope John Paul II has emphasized Mary's singular cooperation in the Redemption (cf. ibid., pp. 217-227).

(105) *Art. cit.*

(106) John Paul II, *Allocution*, in *Insegnamenti di Giovanni Paolo II*, vol. 1, 1978, (Rome: Libreria Editrice Vaticana 1979), p. 250.

(107) John Paul II, *Allocution*, in *L'Osservatore Romano*, Monday-Tuesday, September 19-20, 1994, pp. 6-7.

(108) John Paul II, *Allocution*, September 26, 1982.

(109) Cf. M. Hauke, *La Mediazione materna di Maria secondo Papa Giovanni Paolo II*, p. 86.

(110) John Paul II, *Allocution*, Wroclaw, Poland, June 21, 1983.

(111) John Paul II, Homily, in *L'Osservatore Romano*, Sunday, August 26, 2001, p. 5.

(112) Congregation for the Clergy, *Il presbitero, pastore e guida della comunità parrocchiale*, Istruzione del 4 agosto 2002, Figlie di San Paolo, Milano 2002, p. 82. (English: "Parish Priest's Prayer to Mary Most Holy," in (an appendix to) Congregation for the Clergy, *The Priest, Pastor and Leader of the Parish Community*, Instruction of August 4, 2002 (Vatican City: Libreria Editrice Vaticana, 2002), pp. 53-55.)

(113) Cf. Congregation for Divine Worship, *Decree*, prot. N. 309/86, August 15, 1986, in Conferenza Episcopale Italiana, *Messe della Beata Vergine Maria*, Libreria Editrice Vaticana, Città del Vaticano 1989 (3rd reprint), pp. X-XI.

(114) *Messe della beata Vergine Maria*, op. cit. p. 101. (English cit. by A.B. Calkins, "Mary as Coredemptrix, Mediatrix and Advocate in the Liturgy," in *Mary Coredemptrix Mediatrix Advocate: Theological Foundations. Towards a Papal Definition?* ed. M. Miravalle (Santa Barbara, CA, Queenship, 1995), p. 89.)

(115) *Ibid.*

(116) *Messa di Santa Maria Madre del Signore. Prefazio*, in *Messe della Beata Vergine Maria*, op. cit., p. 66; *Messa di Maria Vergine regina e madre della misericordia. Prefazio*, in op. cit., p. 128; *Messa di Maria*

Vergine Madre della Divina Provvidenza. Prefazio, in op. cit., p. 131.

(117) John Paul II, general audience, *Saluto agli ammalati*, December 10, 1980, in *L'Osservatore Romano*, Thursday, December 11, 1980, p. 2.

(118) Benedict XVI, homily at canonization Mass of Fr. Antônio de Sant'ana Galvão, O.F.M., May 11, 2007, n. 5.

(119) *Ibid.*, n. 6.

(120) For general historical information on this question see J. Schug, *Mary Mother*, cit.; I. Gomá y Thomás, *Estudios y escritos pastoralos sobre la Virgen*, Barcelona 1947. For a classic exposition of the neo-Thomistic pre-conciliar Mariology cf. G. Roschini, *De natura B.M. Virginis in applicatione redemptionis, in Maria et Ecclesia*, vol. II, Rome 1959, pp. 223-295; also P. Parrotta, *La Mariologia di Gabriele Roschini*, Lugano 2002. For a recent approach from a Scotistic point of view, see P.D. Fehlner, F.I., *Mater et Magistra Apostolorum*, in *Immaculata Mediatrix* 1 (1/2001) 15-95; Idem, *De Metaphysica Mariana Quaedam*, in *Immaculata Mediatrix* 1 (2/2002) 13-42; Idem, *Scientia et Pietas*, in *Immaculata Mediatrix* 1 (3/2001) 11-48; Idem, *Io sono L'Immacolata Concezione. Adhuc quaedam de Metaphysica Mariana*, in *Immaculata Mediatrix* 2 (2002) 15-41. Significant contributions to a renewed Thomistic approach have been made by the Spanish metaphysical Mariologist, J. Ferrer Arellano, *La Mediación Materna de la Immacolada. Esperienza Ecumenica de la Iglesia*, Madrid 2006. See also his *Marian Coredemption and Sacramental Mediation*, in *Mary at the Foot of the Cross III*, New Bedford, MA, 2003, pp. 70-126; Idem, *The Immaculate Conception as the Condition for the Possibility of the Coredemption*, in *Mary at the Foot of the Cross V* New Bedford, MA, 2005, pp. 74-185.

(121) Cf. especially the Spanish Dominican, A. Bandera, *La Virgen María y los Sacramentos* (Madrid 1978), and above all the recent study of Serafino M. Lanzetta, F.I., *Il sacerdozio di Maria nella teologia cattolica del XX seculo. Analizi storico-teologica*, Rome 2006. In English, cf. J. Samaha, *The Sacerdotal Quality of Mary's Mission. Mother and Associate of Christ the Priest*, in *Immaculata Mediatrix* 2 (2002) 197-207.

(122) Benedict XVI, *Homily for the Solemnity of the Annunciation*, 2006, insists on the central importance of the Marian principle of the Church, viz., the maternal mediation of Mary at the heart of the Church, and in particular its pastors, and affirms that this mystery was repeatedly underscored by his predecessor, John

Paul II, in accord with his motto, *Totus tuus.*

(123) For texts of St. Maximilian on this subject, see P.D. Fehlner, F.I., *St. Maximilian M. Kolbe, Martyr of Charity, Pneumatologist. His Theology of the Holy Spirit*, New Bedford, MA, 2004.

(124) St. Bonaventure, *III Sent.*, d 3, p 1, a 1, q 2 : "The Virgin Mother is our Mediatrix with Christ as Christ is our Mediator with the Father."; Henry d'Avranches, *Legenda versificata S. Francisci*, in almost the same words describes the spirituality of St. Francis of Assisi.: *Analecta Franciscana*, vol. X, Quaracchi 1941, pp. 405-491, here p. 445.

(125) See Fehlner, *Mater et Magistra Apostolorum*, op cit.

(126) Odo of Canterbury, *Maria Christianorum Philosophia*, ed. by J. Leclercq, in *Mèlanges de science religieuse* 13 (1956) 103-106.

(127) Cf. St. Bonaventure, *III Sent.*, d 3, p 1, a 1, q 1, ad 4: Mariae nullus nimis potest esse devotus.

CHAPTER SIX

ACT OF CONSECRATION TO MARY, MEDIATRIX OF ALL GRACES

Hail, Holy Queen of Heaven and earth; Co-Redemptrix with Christ; Mediatrix of all Grace and Mercy; Advocate for the People of God; Woman clothed with the Sun (cf. Rev 12:1); Spouse of the Holy Spirit; and Spiritual Mother of all humanity (cf. Jn 19:26); we, the Apostles of Light of your Immaculate Heart, come before you this day to renew, through, with and in that same glorious Heart, the solemn vows made at our baptism. We firmly reject Satan, the ancient serpent (cf. Rev 12:9), the Father of Lies, and a murderer from the beginning (cf. Jn 8:44), whose head, swollen with pride, shall be crushed beneath your heel (cf. Gen 3:15), and of whose poison cup we refuse to drink; we reject this world and its vanities, of which the devil is prince (cf. Jn 12:31); finally, we reject every form of impurity of mind and heart, body and soul, intellect, will and spirit.

In the presence of the Most High Triune God and His cloud of heavenly witnesses (cf. Heb 12:1-2), the angels and saints, we take you, O Blessed Virgin Mary, as our Spiritual Mother (cf. Jn 19:26); and, taking to heart what has been said of you – "she will meet him as an honourable mother, and will receive him as a wife married of a virgin. With the bread of life...she shall feed him, and give him the water of wholesome wisdom to drink: and she shall be made strong in him, and he shall not be moved" (cf. Sir 15:1-2) – we hereby espouse your Immaculate Heart, offering to you, O Mary, our little Hearts, so full of sin and self-love; that you, who cannot and will not be outdone in liberality and generosity, might meet us in the same spirit and offer to us your own Immaculate Heart. Furthermore, may we participate in your own fullness of grace, and be clothed with the myriad virtues and merits that adorn the glorious temple of your Holy Heart. Please obtain for us a deep, ever-increasing spousal intimacy of life with you, in order that by being ever more united with, and conformed to, your Immaculate Heart, in imitation of St. Joseph – our exemplar and Universal Patron - we might become increasingly united with, and conformed to, the Sacred and Eucharistic Heart of Our Lord, Jesus Christ – your Son and our Lord – such that we might adore His Heart with the perfect, unadulterated and immaculate love of your own Immaculate Heart, and thereby be found pleasing in His sight.

Thus, we solemnly entrust and consecrate to you, O Immaculate Virgin Mary, in our abject misery, poverty, weakness, sinfulness and nothingness, everything that we are and have, just as we are, without reserve: body, soul, intellect, will and emotions; all of our interior and exterior goods and possessions; and even the satisfactory, meritorious value of all our good works – past, present and future – for you to dispose of according to the designs of your Immaculate Heart, in anticipation of the promised Triumph of your Immaculate Heart in the Church and the world, and in preparation for the long-awaited establishment of the holy city, the new Jerusalem, that shall come down out of heaven, and through which all creation shall return to the perfect glorification of God, Who shall establish His glorious kingdom on earth and dwelling amongst men, having conquered and crushed the head of the ancient serpent. (cf. Rev 21:2-3).

Like lambs led to the slaughter who open not their mouths (cf. Acts 8:32), we place ourselves and the spiritual sacrifice of our prayers, works, joys, and especially our sufferings – of this day and of our entire lives – on the altar of your Immaculate Heart. Please, Holy Mother, unite us and our offerings to Jesus and His perfect offering of Himself, renewed this day and every day, throughout the world, from the rising of the sun to its setting, to the perfect glorification of God.

As members of Christ's Mystical Body and participants in His Royal Priesthood, a dignity and office bestowed upon all the baptized, may our daily participation in the Holy Sacrifice of the Mass be the center of our day and the center of our lives. As the true re-presentation of the once-for-all sacrifice accomplished by Christ on Calvary, may we be ever-increasingly aware of this truly awesome reality in which we participate, and by which we are united and sanctified.

Thus, we offer this sacrifice in a profound act of glorification, adoration, gratitude, reparation and supplication to the Most Holy Trinity; for the intentions and the consolation of the Two Sacred Hearts of Jesus and Mary; for the Church's solemn recognition and definition of Your Spiritual Motherhood, Mary; for the Holy Father and his intentions; for all bishops, priests, deacons and religious of the One, Holy, Catholic and Apostolic Church; for an increase in vocations to the holy, ministerial priesthood of Christ Jesus; for all God's priestly people; and for the salvation of all souls until the end of time.

In imitation of Christ, your dearly beloved Son, "the firstborn of all creation" (cf. Col 1:15), we humbly request that the chalice of suffering might be taken from us (cf. Lk 22:42); yet, with Christ and in imitation of you, O Holy Virgin, we ultimately submit our unconditional and irrevocable fiat to the Divine Will, as we echo Christ's prayer of obedient resignation: "Father, if thou wilt, remove this chalice from me: but yet not my will, but thine be done" (Lk 22:42); and we patiently accept, in advance, those unavoidable crosses and sufferings that the Divine

Heart of God, in His infinite and inscrutable wisdom, has pre-ordained for each; understanding that the salvation of the many is contingent upon the sanctification of the few. O Mother and Mediatrix of all Grace and Mercy, may we truly participate in Your fullness of Grace and be clothed with your own heroic virtues of faith, hope, charity, purity, humility, poverty of spirit, littleness, hiddenness, fortitude, and that perfect resignation of will necessary to deny our very selves, pick up our crosses daily, and follow Jesus (cf. Lk 9:23) on the narrow path of evangelical poverty, chastity and obedience; bearing witness to our faith in Christ and His Holy Gospel in all of our thoughts, words and deeds, even to the point of the shedding of our blood, should we be called to wear the holy crown of martyrdom.

And when our mission on this earth has been accomplished, we pray that, through the most powerful intercession of St. Joseph, Universal Patron and Patron of the Dying, we too might be personally escorted, by Jesus and Mary, to the throne of the Thrice Holy Godhead; that the Eternal Father, seeing reproduced in our souls the image of His crucified Christ, might invite us to the Eternal Banquet, the heavenly wedding feast of the Lamb and His Bride, the Church (cf. Rev 19:9). Furthermore, having comprised the humble "heel" of the Mystical Body used by you, Mary, to crush the head of the ancient serpent (cf. Gen: 3:15), may we, one day, make up bright, shining stars in the crown about your Most Immaculate Heart (cf. Rev 12:1). And may we behold He Who is, Who was, and Who shall be for all eternity, participating in the merits of the angels and saints in paradise and in the eternal chorus of praise, glory, wisdom, thanks, honor, power and might to our God forever and ever (cf. Rev 7:12). Amen.

PART II
LIVING ONE'S CONSECRATION

CHAPTER SEVEN

THE HOLY ROSARY

A **Crown of Roses About Her Most Immaculate Heart**

Second only to the most Holy Sacrifice of the Mass, the Rosary of our Blessed Lady is, without question, the "highest" and "most exalted" form of Catholic prayer, and this due to the fact that we meditate on the central mysteries of Christ's life, death and resurrection, through, with and in the Immaculate Heart of Mary, she who " kept all these [mysteries], pondering them in her heart" (Lk 2:19). Moreover, it appears as though this exalted form of Christian prayer was prophetically announced in the Old Testament Book of Ecclesiasticus (or Sirach),

Chapter 24, Verse 18, where "Created Wisdom," a figure of the Blessed Virgin Mary, states the following of herself: "I am the mother of fair love, and fear, and knowledge, and holy hope." This single passage certainly seems to be a most appropriate description of each of the four sets of mysteries, as the Joyful Mysteries can be characterized as expressive of the *fair love* of our Lord and our Lady; the Sorrowful Mysteries teach us to *fear* the re-crucifixion of Christ through the commission of sin; the Luminous Mysteries shed the light of *knowledge* on the public mysteries of Christ's three-year ministry; and, finally, the Glorious mysteries teach us to hold onto the *holy hope* that this set of mysteries sets before the eyes of our soul.

Certainly, saints, popes and mystics have all spoken as highly as possible of this most salutary form of prayer. We do well to briefly examine just a few of the many wonderous things that have been said of the Holy Rosary, by some of the greatest popes, clergy, religious and laity alike, who, through their devotion to this most holy prayer, were capable of attaining, for themselves and others, great and lofty degrees of holiness and sanctification:

"Continue to pray the Rosary every day." -**Our Lady of Fatima to Sister Lucia**

"Never will anyone who says his Rosary every day be led astray. This is a statement that I would gladly sign with my blood. **-Saint Louis de Montfort**

"You shall obtain all you ask of me by the recitation

of the Rosary." **-Our Lady to Blessed Alan de la Roche**

"Give me an army saying the Rosary and I will conquer the world." **-Pope Blessed Pius IX**

"If you persevere in reciting the Rosary, this will be a most probable sign of your eternal salvation." **Blessed Alan de la Roche**

"The greatest method of praying is to pray the Rosary."
-Saint Francis de Sales

"When the Holy Rosary is said well, it gives Jesus and Mary more glory and is more meritorious than any other prayer." **-Saint Louis de Montfort**

"The Holy Rosary is the storehouse of countless blessing." **-Blessed Alan de la Roche**

"One day, through the Rosary and the Scapular, Our Lady will save the world." -**Saint Dominic**

"If you say the Rosary faithfully unto death, I do assure you that, in spite of the gravity of your sins, 'you will receive a never-fading crown of glory' (1 St. Peter 5:4)." -**Saint Louis de Montfort**

"You must know that when you 'hail' Mary, she immediately greets you! Don't think that she is one of those rude women of whom there are so many—on the contrary, she is utterly courteous and pleasant. If you greet her, she will answer you right away and converse with you!" -**Saint Bernardine of Siena**

"Recite your Rosary with faith, with humility, with confidence, and with perseverance." -**Saint Louis de Montfort**

"The Rosary is the most beautiful and the most rich in graces of all prayers; it is the prayer that touches most the Heart of the Mother of God...and if you wish peace to reign in your homes, recite the family Rosary." -**Pope Saint Pius X**

"Never will anyone who says his Rosary every day become a formal heretic or be led astray by the devil." -**Saint Louis de Montfort**

"Even if you are on the brink of damnation, even if you have one foot in hell, even if you have sold your soul to the devil as sorcerers do who practice black magic, and even if you are a heretic as obstinate as a devil, sooner or later you will be converted and will amend your life and will save your soul, if—and mark well what I say—if you say the Holy Rosary devoutly every day until death for the purpose of knowing the truth and obtaining contrition and pardon for your sins." -**Saint Louis de Montfort**

"The Most Holy Virgin in these last times in which we live has given a new efficacy to the recitation of the Rosary to such an extent that there is no problem, no matter how difficult it is, whether temporal or above all spiritual, in the personal life of each one of us, of our families...that cannot be solved by the

Rosary. There is no problem, I tell you, no matter how difficult it is, that we cannot resolve by the prayer of the Holy Rosary." -**Sister Lucia dos Santos, Fatima seer**

"When you say your Rosary, the angels rejoice, the Blessed Trinity delights in it, my Son finds joy in it too, and I myself am happier than you can possibly guess. After the Holy Sacrifice of the Mass, there is nothing in the Church that I love as much as the Rosary." -**Our Lady to Blessed Alan de la Roche**

"'Hail Mary, full of grace, the Lord is with thee!' No creature has ever said anything that was more pleasing to me, nor will anyone ever be able to find or say to me anything that pleases me more." -**Our Lady to Saint Mechtilde**

(c.f.: http://www.tfp.org/quotes-of-our-lady-popes-and-saints/)

In each well-prayed Rosary, the Mother truly unites her most beautiful and all-powerful voice to ours, making of our prayer a truly pleasing and fragrant offering unto each of the persons of the Most Holy Trinity. In it, the Father rejoices in receiving sublime consolation from His creation through the Immaculate Heart of the Mother of His Son; the Son eagerly presses to His Most Sacred Heart all hearts that have been entrusted and offered to Him by His Most Holy Mother; the Spirit, or the Divine Advocate, is irresistibly drawn to each soul in whom His well-beloved spouse, the created Advocate – Mary – has made her dwelling. Finally, it goes without saying that our Spiritual Mother leaps with joy each and every time she is greeted, by one of her many beloved children, in the same manner that she was greeted by St. Gabriel, who, in announcing to her the exalted vocation to which she had been called by God, greeted her with that sweet "Ave." Thus, after the supremely perfect glory and honor offered to God in the Liturgical celebration of the Holy Sacrifice of the Mass, it would not be an exaggeration to state that the Holy Trinity receives its greatest adoration, glorification, gratitude, supplication and expiation from those individuals who, through, with and in the Immaculate Heart of Mary, the masterpiece of God's creation and the treasury of God's greatest graces, allow themselves to be transformed ever more perfectly into Christ's image and likeness through their meditation on the salvific mysteries of Christ's life, death and resurrection, as they repeat the words of the Angelic Salutation (the Hail Mary).

The Rosary involves both meditative and vocal prayer, and quite often leads one into a passive state of contemplation, whereby the soul ceases to be active, but rather rests in the peace, love and, above all, the very presence of God Himself.

We must, however, first understand the critical distinction between meditation and contemplation. The former (meditation) involves activity on our part; that is, as we meditate on any of the 20 mysteries of the Rosary, we simultaneously pray out loud, vocally (or, at least, mouth the words silently, to ourselves, as must be done when in a public place of worship, such as a church or a Eucharistic Chapel), to Our Lady, rendering unto her the praise and veneration that is Her due, and asking her to exercise her maternal mediation on our behalf.

Contemplative prayer, on the other hand, is a free gift bestowed upon an individual who is properly disposed to receive this gift. We prepare ourselves precisely by performing the activities of both vocal and meditative prayer. Contemplation can be defined as the passive, phenomenological, subjective experience of the soul resting in the presence of God. Moreover, it should be noted that we do not pray in order to receive this free gift of contemplative prayer; God may or may not choose to impart this gift upon a soul, knowing, in His perfect Wisdom, precisely what each individual soul needs at any given time. Rather, we, having committed ourselves to the Blessed Virgin, have promised to stay united to her Most Immaculate Heart, and this is accomplished through, with and in the recitation of her prayer, the Most Holy Rosary, and active meditation on the Paschal Mystery, which includes the Incarnation, Life, Passion, Death, Resurrection and Ascencion of our Lord; the sacred mysteries of our salvation.

As we read above, countless saints, mystics and popes have hailed the Rosary of our Blessed Mother the single most salutary and efficacious of devotions after Holy Mass, and the Mother of God herself has come from heaven to reveal the treasures of grace hidden in the Rosary. In every single Church-approved apparition of Our Lady during the 20th Century, she admonishes us to pray this, her prayer. Despite what has already been stated, we might still be wondering why the Rosary, in particular, is so powerful. The answer is quite simple: not unlike our mysterious Lord, Who is, simultaneously, profoundly simple and infinitely profound, so too is the prayer of the Holy Rosary. It is so simple that the youngest of children can be taught to pray it; yet the mysteries that are meditated upon are, in all truth and without the least exaggeration, "mysteries" in the strictest sense of the word; that is, they are truths belonging to the Sacred Deposit of Faith that surpass the finite, limited human mind's ability to grasp their full import. In truth, these mysteries are literally inexhaustible. It is precisely for this reason that such brilliant minds as those of Aquinas and John Paul II were capable of speaking of the inestimable value the repeated recitation of the "Angelic Salutation" while meditating upon the mysteries of God's salvific plan for humanity.

As Catholic Christians, the Most Holy Rosary of Our Lady truly is among the most powerful of weapons we possess as we wage war with Satan for souls. The prayer of the Rosary can, quite literally, alter world events: it can prevent world wars, put an end to the silent holocaust of abortion, bring about the conversion of even the most hardened of sinners and enemies of Holy Mother Church, and, most importantly, hasten the promised "Triumph of the Immaculate Heart of Mary" in the world, thereby ushering in the new era, the new springtime for the Church and the world, with all of creation returning to the perfect glorification of the Lord, its creator.

Moreover, the daily prayer of the Holy Rosary is absolutely integral to the living of one's total consecration to Mary, as is the wearing of Our Lady's religious habit or garment of the Brown Scapular (truly the "religious habit" of those souls consecrated to Our Lady and her service) for it is simultaneously the chain that (1) binds us to Mary's Most Immaculate Heart, whose Heart beats in a perfect union of love with the Sacred Heart of Christ Jesus, her Son and her God; (2) and it is additionally the chain that shall forever bind Satan, or Lucifer, in the everlasting lake of fire, thereby preventing him from prowling throughout the world in his endless effort to bring souls created by God and for God to ultimate ruin. Thus, the Rosary can be thought of as the "key" that unlocks the door of and gains us entrance into the glorious temple and refuge of Mary's Immaculate Heart. One who is consecrated to the Immaculate Heart of Mary should, in keeping with one's total dedication and gift of self to Mary Immaculate through their solemn act of consecration, commit him/herself to the praying of *at least* five decades of the Rosary daily. Ideally, we should strive to pray an entire 15 or 20 decade Rosary daily.

Finally, the Rosary holds a place of particular importance in these most difficult times through which we are living; specifically, that period of time spoken of in the last book of Sacred Scripture, the Book of Revelation. For, as the Eternal Father's demand for Divine Justice escalates, and chastisements increase in frequency, duration and intensity, the Holy Rosary shall become our only refuge and our sole source of strength, endurance and survival.

The Traditional Dominican Rosary

The traditional Dominican Rosary of Our Lady is composed of five sets of ten small beads, separated by 5 large beads. Each bead on the small set of 10 represents one "Hail Mary." The "Our Father" is prayed on the large beads.

Meditation on the Mysteries of the Holy Rosary constitute the "heart" of this devotion. Traditionally, there were three sets of Mysteries; the Joyful, the Sorrowful and the Glorious. Toward the end of his pontificate, Blessed Pope John Paul II made a marvelous contribution to the history of the Rosary by adding a fourth set of mysteries, the "Mysteries of Light," or the "Luminous Mysteries."

The Five Joyful Mysteries, traditionally prayed on Monday and Saturday:

1. The Annunciation; 2. The Visitation; 3. The Nativity; 4. The Presentation of Our Lord in the Temple; 5. The Finding of Jesus in the Temple.

The Five Sorrowful Mysteries, traditionally prayed on Tuesday and Friday:

1. The Agony in the Garden; 2. The Scourging at the Pillar; 3. The Crowning with Thorns; 4. The Carrying of the Cross; 5. The Crucifixion.

The Five Glorious Mysteries, traditionally prayed on Wednesday and Sunday:

1. The Resurrection; 2. The Ascension; 3. The Decent of the Holy Spirit at Pentecost; 4. The Assumption of Mary, Body and Soul, into Heaven; 5. The Coronation of Mary as Queen of Heaven and Earth.

The Five Luminous Mysteries, now prayed on Thursday:

1. The Baptism of Jesus; 2. The Wedding at Cana; 3. Proclaiming the Kingdom of God; 4. The Transfiguration; 5. The Eucharist.

How To Pray The Rosary In Ten Steps

(1) Begin by making the "Sign of the Cross" with the Crucifix in hand. While holding the Crucifix, recite the *Apostles Creed*: "I believe in God the Father Almighty, Creator of Heaven and earth; and in Jesus Christ, His only Son, our Lord, Who was conceived by the Holy Spirit, born of the Virgin Mary, suffered under Pontius Pilate, was crucified, died and was buried; He descended into hell; the third day He arose again from the dead; He ascended into Heaven, and is seated at the right hand of God, the Father Almighty; From thence He shall come to judge the living and the dead. I believe in the Holy Spirit, the Holy Catholic Church, the Communion of Saints, the forgiveness of sins, the resurrection of the body, and

life everlasting. Amen."

(2) On the first bead recite the *Our Father*: "Our Father Who art in Heaven, hallowed be Thy Name; Thy kingdom come; Thy will be done on earth as it is in Heaven. Give us this day our daily bread, and forgive us our trespasses, as we forgive those who trespass against us, and lead us not into temptation, but deliver us from evil. Amen."

(3) On the three small beads recite the *Hail Mary* for an increase in the supernatural virtues of Faith, Hope and Charity: "Hail Mary, full of grace, the Lord is with thee; blessed art thou among women, and blessed is the fruit of thy womb, Jesus. Holy Mary, Mother of God, pray for us sinners, now and at the hour of our death. Amen."

(4) Recite the *Glory Be*: "Glory be to the Father, and to the Son, and to the Holy Ghost, as it was in the beginning, is now, and ever shall be, world without end. Amen."

(5) Call to mind the Mystery, then on the large bead recite the *Our Father*.

(6) On the ten small beads recite the *Hail Mary* while meditating on the mystery.

(7) Recite the *Glory Be*.

(8) After the *Glory Be*, recite the *Fatima Prayer*: "O my Jesus, forgive us our sins. Save us from the fires of

hell. Lead all souls into heaven, especially those in most need of thy mercy."

(9) Repeat steps 5-8 until you have completed the five decades of the Rosary.

(10) Conclude the Rosary by praying the *Salve Regina*: "Hail, Holy Queen, Mother of Mercy, our life, our sweetness, and our hope; to Thee do we come, poor banished children of Eve; to Thee do we send up our sighs, mourning and weeping in this vale of tears. Turn, then, most gracious Advocate, Thine eyes of mercy toward us, and after this, our exile, show unto us the most blessed fruit of Thy womb, Jesus, O clement, O loving, O sweet Virgin Mary."

The Scriptural Rosary

Many persons find it difficult to keep their attention fixed on the mysteries that are supposed to be meditated upon while praying the *Hail Mary* prayers. A most effective method of facilitating one's ability to meditate upon the mystery is by praying the *Scriptural Rosary*. In the Scriptural Rosary, a passage from Sacred Scripture is recited immediately prior to the praying of the *Hail Mary*. Many persons, including this author, have found that by meditating on a select passage from Scripture with each Hail Mary, the overall experience of the praying of the Holy Rosary of Our Lady is greatly enhanced and deeply enriching. Moreover, having a new passage to meditate on with each Hail Mary not only helps us to stay focused on the mystery, but additionally breaks up the "monotony" of reciting the same prayers again and again. This author would absolutely suggest the Scriptural Rosary to anyone who would like to enhance their experience of the praying of the Holy Rosary.

My greatest hope and prayer is that you, the reader, will find that "praying," and not simply "saying," the Holy Rosary truly facilitates a deep, profound and life-changing encounter with the living Word of God, the Logos, the Second Person of the Most Holy Trinity, Jesus, the Christ, and His Most Holy Mother, our true Spiritual Mother, Mary Immaculate.

The 15 Promises for those who recite the Rosary

(1) Whoever shall faithfully serve me by the recitation of the rosary, shall receive signal graces.

(2) I promise my special protection and the greatest graces to all those who shall recite the rosary.

(3) The rosary shall be a powerful armor against hell, it will destroy vice, decrease sin, and defeat heresies.

(4) It will cause virtue and good works to flourish; it will obtain for souls the abundant mercy of God; it will withdraw the heart of men from the love of the world and its vanities, and will lift them to the desire of eternal things. Oh, that souls would sanctify themselves by this means.

(5) The soul which recommends itself to me by the recitation of the rosary shall not perish.

(6) Whoever shall recite the rosary devoutly, applying himself to the consideration of its sacred mysteries, shall never be conquered by misfortune. God will not chastise him in His justice, he shall not perish by an unprovided death; if he be just he shall remain in the grace of God, and become worthy of eternal life.

(7) Whoever shall have a true devotion for the rosary shall not die without the sacraments of the Church.

(8) Those who are faithful to recite the rosary shall have during their life and at their death the light of God and the plenitude of His graces; at the moment of death they shall participate in the merits of the saints in paradise.

(9) I shall deliver from purgatory those who have been devoted to the rosary.

(10) The faithful children of the rosary shall merit a high degree of glory in heaven.

(11) You shall obtain all you ask of me by the recitation of the rosary.

(12) All those who propagate the holy rosary shall be aided by me in their necessities.

(13) I have obtained from my Divine Son that all the advocates of the rosary shall have for intercessors the entire celestial court during their life and at the hour of death.

(14) All who recite the rosary are my sons, and brothers of my only son Jesus Christ.

(15) Devotion of my rosary is a great sign of predestination.

CHAPTER EIGHT

MARIAN PRAYER CENACLES

What Is A Marian Prayer Cenacle, And Why Should We Promote Them?

The Blessed Mother, in her many visitations and apparitions throughout the world, is specifically requesting that the faithful come together in cenacles of prayer through, with and in her, in order to invoke a new, "Second Pentecost;" that Mary's Divine Spouse, the Holy Spirit of God, might come again, just as He did during that first Pentecost, which is chronicled in Acts 2:1-47, and has been reproduced below.

Moreover, Our Lady, in numerous private revelations and messages, has promised to be present in an especially substantial fashion, with her glorified body, during these cenacles of prayer. In fact, it is not at all uncommon for persons to receive beautiful signal graces and supernatural signs and confirmations of Our Lady's presence amongst her children during such gatherings of prayer offered to God through her. Some of the signs of Our Lady's presence are the scent of roses where there are no roses present; the chain and other metal pieces of one's rosary inexplicably changing from the original silver color to a gold color; the ability to stare into the sun while witnessing various solar miracles, similar to the solar miracle which took place on October 13, 1917, during the last apparition of Our Lady at Fatima; statues and images of the Blessed Mother and other saints seemingly "weeping" tears of water, rose-scented oil, or, in some rare instances, tears of human blood; instances of statues of the Blessed Virgin that appear to come alive or change hue or color; the miraculous manifestation / materialization of rose petals, etc. Contrary to the beliefs of many persons, even deeply spiritual persons, such occurrences are extremely common at the numerous places throughout the world where Our Lady is currently appearing. Moreover, Our Lady, according to one of her messages given to Fr. Gobbi of the Marian Movement of Priests, claims that she is currently appearing on every continent throughout the world, and that these are some of the many signs that accompany and lend credibility to the apparitions that she is making and that certain persons are reporting.

Typical Structure of a Marian Prayer Cenacle

A Cenacle must have a minimum of two persons, but may be as large as a soccer stadium full of people!

Essentially, the more persons present, the better. We offer the following outline as a suggested format for a traditional Marian Prayer Cenacle. The outline has intentionally been left vague and without specific prayers, in order that individuals developing Cenacles of their own may be open to the promptings of the Spirit regarding the specific prayers that they believe ought to be used. The general format, however, almost always should include the following:

- Introductory prayer to the Holy Spirit;
- Prayers for the Holy Father, for all priests, and for the Church, that it might withstand all of the many and varied attacks that are daily made upon it from both within and without;
- Recitation of the Holy Rosary (at least 5 decades);
- A reading taken from one of the four Gospels, or, possibly, the Gospel reading either for that day or the upcoming or previous Sunday;
- A Mariological Reading/Reflection that may be taken from a variety of sources, such as the writings of any of the saints on Mary; passages from St. Louis de Montfort's "True Devotion to Mary;" the Marian writings and reflections of St. Maximilian Kolbe; passages from "The Glories of Mary" or "The City of God;" Church/Magisterial teachings on Mary; Pope St. John Paul's Marian Encyclical Letter, "Redemptoris Mater;" private revelations that have received a nihil obstat and/or an Imprimatur, which is an official Church declaration that the document contains nothing that is contrary to the faith;

- Recitation of the Chaplet of Divine Mercy;
- Intercessory prayers;
- Group recitation and renewal of a solemn Act of Consecration to the Immaculate Heart of Mary;
- Closing prayers to the Trinity and prayers of thanksgiving.

The Holy Spirit Comes at Pentecost in the First Cenacle with Our Lady (Acts 2:1-47)

"When the day of Pentecost came, they were all together in one place. Suddenly a sound like the blowing of a violent wind came from heaven and filled the whole house where they were sitting. They saw what seemed to be tongues of fire that separated and came to rest on each of them. All of them were filled with the Holy Spirit and began to speak in other tongues as the Spirit enabled them.

"Now there were staying in Jerusalem God-fearing Jews from every nation under heaven. When they heard this sound, a crowd came together in bewilderment, because each one heard them speaking in his own language. Utterly amazed, they asked: "Are not all these men who are speaking Galileans? Then how is it that each of us hears them in his own native language? Parthians, Medes and Elamites; residents of Mesopotamia, Judea and Cappadocia, Pontus and Asia, Phrygia and Pamphylia, Egypt and the parts of Libya near Cyrene; visitors from Rome (both Jews and converts to Judaism); Cretans and Arabs—we hear them declaring the wonders of God in our own tongues!" Amazed and perplexed, they asked one another, "What does this mean?" Some, however, made fun of them and said, "They have had too much wine."

Peter Addresses the Crowd

"Then Peter stood up with the Eleven, raised his voice and addressed the crowd: "Fellow Jews and all of you who live in Jerusalem, let me explain this to you; listen carefully to what I say. These men are not drunk, as you suppose. It's only nine in the morning! No, this is what was spoken by the prophet Joel: "'In the last days, God says, I will pour out my Spirit on all people. Your sons and daughters will prophesy, your young men will see visions, your old men will dream dreams. Even on my servants, both men and women, I will pour out my Spirit in those days, and they will prophesy. I will show wonders in the heaven above and signs on the earth below, blood and fire and billows of smoke. The sun will be turned to darkness and the moon to blood before the coming of the great and glorious day of the Lord. And everyone who calls on the name of the Lord will be saved.'

"Men of Israel, listen to this: Jesus of Nazareth was a man accredited by God to you by miracles, wonders and signs, which God did among you through him, as you yourselves know. This man was handed over to you by God's set purpose and foreknowledge; and you, with the help of wicked men, put him to death by nailing him to the cross. But God raised him from the dead, freeing him from the agony of death, because it was impossible for death to keep its hold on him. David said about him:

"'I saw the Lord always before me. Because he is at my right hand, I will not be shaken. Therefore my heart is glad and my tongue rejoices; my body also will live in hope, because you will not abandon me to the grave, nor will you let your Holy One see decay. You have made known to me the paths of life;you will fill me with joy in your presence.' "Brothers, I can tell you confidently that the patriarch David died and was buried, and his tomb is here to this day. But he was a prophet and knew that God had promised him on oath that he would place one of his descendants on his throne. Seeing what was ahead, he spoke of the resurrection of the Christ, that he was not abandoned to the grave, nor did his body see decay. God has raised this Jesus to life, and we are all witnesses of the fact. Exalted to the right hand of God, he has received from the Father the promised Holy Spirit and has poured out what you now see and hear. For David did not ascend to heaven, and yet he said, "'The Lord said to my Lord: "Sit at my right hand until I make your enemies a footstool for your feet.""' "Therefore let all Israel be assured of this: God has made this Jesus, whom you crucified, both Lord and Christ." When the people heard this, they were cut to the heart and said to Peter and the other apostles, "Brothers, what shall we do?" Peter replied, "Repent and be baptized, every one of you, in the name of Jesus Christ for the forgiveness of your sins. And you will receive the gift of the Holy Spirit. The promise is for you and your children and for all who are far off—for all whom the Lord our God will call."

"With many other words he warned them; and he pleaded with them, "Save yourselves from this corrupt generation." Those who accepted his message were baptized, and about three thousand were added to their number that day.

The Fellowship of the Believers

"They devoted themselves to the apostles' teaching and to the fellowship, to the breaking of bread and to prayer. Everyone was filled with awe, and many wonders and miraculous signs were done by the apostles. All the believers were together and had everything in common. Selling their possessions and goods, they gave to anyone as he had need. Every day they continued to meet together in the temple courts. They broke bread in their homes and ate together with glad and sincere hearts, praising God and enjoying the favor of all the people. And the Lord added to their number daily those who were being saved (Acts 2:1-47).

CHAPTER NINE

SUGGESTED CENACLE PRAYERS AND FORMAT

Opening Prayer to the Holy Spirit

Come, Holy Spirit, fill the hearts of thy Faithful;
and enkindle in them the fire of Thy love.
Send forth Thy Spirit and they shall be created,
and thou shalt renew the face of the earth.

Let us pray.

O God, who didst instruct the hearts of the faithful
by the light of the Holy Spirit, grant us in the same
Spirit to be truly wise and ever to rejoice in His consolation. through the same Christ our Lord.

Amen.

Daily Prayer to the Holy Spirit

O Holy Spirit, beloved of my soul, I adore You.
Enlighten me, guide me, strengthen me, console me.
Tell me what I should do; give me Your orders.
I promise to submit myself to all that You desire of me
and to accept all that You permit to happen to me.
Reveal to me Your Will, and grant me the courage,
strength, determination and resolve to act accordingly, by
cooperating fully with the actual graces that you will supply
for each moment.

Amen.

Prayer to St Joseph

O holy Patriarch, St. Joseph,
I rejoice with you at the exalted dignity
by which you were deemed worthy
to act as Virginal Father to Jesus,
to give Him orders,
and to be obeyed by Him
whom heaven and earth obey!
O great Joseph,
as you were served by God,
I too wish to be taken into your service.
I choose you after Mary to be my chief advocate and

protector.
I promise to honor you every day
by some special act of devotion
and by placing myself under your daily protection.
By that sweet company
which Jesus and Mary gave you in your lifetime,
protect me all through life,
so that I may never separate myself from God
by losing His grace.
My dear Joseph, pray to Jesus for me.
Certainly He can never refuse you anything,
since He obeyed all your orders while on earth.
Ask Him to detach me from all creatures and from myself,
to inflame me with His holy love,
and then to do with me what He pleases.
And by that assistance which Jesus and Mary gave you at
death,
I beg of you to protect me in a special way
at the hour of my death,
so that dying assisted by you,
in the company of Jesus and Mary,
I may go to thank you in heaven,
and in your company to sing God's praises for all eternity.

Amen.

Pray Five Decades of the Holy Rosary.

After the Fatima Prayer, Pray the "Come, Holy Spirit"

Come, Holy Spirit; Come by means of the most powerful
intercession of the Immaculate Heart of Mary, Your Well-
Beloved Spouse.

The Angel of Fatima Prayer

Most Holy Trinity,
Father, Son and Holy Spirit,
I adore Thee profoundly.
I offer Thee the most precious Body, Blood, Soul
and Divinity of Jesus Christ,
present in all the tabernacles of the world,
in reparation for the outrages,
sacrileges and indifferences whereby He is offended.
And through the infinite merits of His Most Sacred Heart
and the Immaculate Heart of Mary,
I beg of Thee the conversion of poor sinners.

The Pardon Prayer

O my God,
I believe,
I adore,
I trust and I love Thee.
I ask pardon for those who do not believe,
do not adore,
do not trust and do not love Thee. (3X)

A Prayer for Priests

O Jesus,
I pray for Your faithful and fervent priests;
for Your unfaithful and tepid priests;
for Your priests labouring at home
or abroad in distant mission fields;
for Your tempted priests;

for Your lonely and desolate priest;
for Your young priests;
for Your dying priests;
for the souls of Your priests in purgatory.
But above all I recommend to You the priests dearest to
me;
the priest who baptized me;
the priests who absolved me from my sins;
the priests at whose Masses I assisted
and who gave me Your Body and Blood in Holy
communion;
the priests who taught and instructed me;
all the priests to whom I am indebted in any other way.
O Jesus, keep them all close to Your heart,
and bless them abundantly in time and in eternity.

Amen.

Act of Faith

O my God,
I firmly believe that you are one God
in three divine Persons,
Father, Son, and Holy Spirit.
I believe that your divine son became man,
died for our sins,
and that he will come to judge the living and the dead.
I believe these and all the truths
which the holy Catholic Church teaches,
because you who have revealed them,
who can neither deceive nor be deceived.

Amen.

Act of Hope

O my God!
Who hast graciously promised every blessing,
even Heaven itself,
through Jesus Christ,
to those who keep Thy commandments;
relying on Thine infinite power,
goodness and mercy,
and confiding in Thy sacred promises,
to which Thou art always faithful,
I confidently hope to obtain pardon of all my sins;
grace to serve Thee faithfully in this life,
by doing the good works Thou hast commanded,
and which,
with Thine assistance,
I now purpose to perform,
and eternal happiness in the next,
through my Lord and Saviour Jesus Christ. Amen.

Act of Charity

O my God, I love You above all things
with my whole heart and soul
because You are all good and worthy of all my love.

I love my neighbor as myself for the love of You.

I forgive all who have injured me
and ask pardon of all whom I have injured.

Amen.

The Confiteor

I confess to Almighty God,
to blessed Mary ever Virgin,
to blessed Michael the Archangel,
to blessed John the Baptist,
to the holy apostles Peter and Paul,
and to all the saints
that I have sinned exceedingly
in thought, word, and deed,
through my fault,
through my fault,
through my most grievous fault.
Therefore, I beseech blessed Mary ever Virgin,
blessed Michael the Archangel,
blessed John the Baptist,
the holy Apostles Peter and Paul,
and all the saints,
to pray for me to the Lord our God.

Amen.

Pray the Divine Mercy Chaplet

To be Prayed on a Regular Five-Decade Rosary

I Opening Prayer

Eternal God,
in whom mercy is endless
and the treasury of compassion
- inexhaustible,

look kindly upon us
and increase Your mercy in us,
that in difficult moments
we might not despair
nor become despondent,
but with great confidence
submit ourselves to Your holy will,
which is Love and Mercy itself.

Amen.

Jesus, I Trust In You! (3X)

II Preliminary Prayers:

Pray one "Our Father," one "Hail Mary," and the
"Apostles Creed"

III Main Prayers

On the "Our Father" Big beads, Pray:

Eternal Father, I offer You the Body and Blood, Soul and
Divinity, of Your Dearly Beloved Son, Our Lord, Jesus
Christ /

In atonement for our sins, and those of the whole world

On the smaller "Hail Mary" beads, Pray:

For the sake of His sorrowful passion /

Have mercy on us, and on the whole world (10X)

Repeat for all Five Decades

At the End of the Last Decade, Recite the following Three Times, in Honor of Each Person of the Trinity

Holy God, Holy Mighty One, Holy Immortal One,

Have Mercy on Us, and On the Whole World (3X)

Prayer

O God, in Whom Mercy is endless, and the treasury of
compassion, inexhaustible; Look kindly upon us, and
increase You Mercy in us; So that, in difficult time we
might not despair, nor become despondent, but with great
confidence, submit ourselves to Your Holy Will, which is
love and Mercy itself.

Jesus, I Trust In You. (3X)

Closing Prayer

O Greatly Merciful God,
Infinite Goodness,
today all mankind calls out from the abyss
of its misery to Your mercy - to Your compassion, O God;
and it is with its mighty voice of misery that it cries out.
Gracious God, do not reject the prayer of this earth's
exiles!
O Lord, Goodness beyond our understanding,
who are acquainted with our misery
through and through and know that by our own power
we cannot ascend to You,
we implore You,

anticipate us with Your grace
and keep on increasing Your mercy in us,
that we may faithfully do Your Holy Will
all through our life and at death's hour.
Let the omnipotence of Your mercy shield us
from the darts of our salvation's enemies,
that we may with confidence,
as Your children,
await Your final coming - that day known to You alone.
And we expect to obtain everything promised us by Jesus
in spite of all our wretchedness.
For Jesus is our Hope;
Through His merciful Heart,
as through an open gate,
we pass through to heaven.

Amen.

Consecration to the Sacred Heart of Jesus

O Sacred Heart of Jesus,
to Thee I consecrate and offer up my person and my life,
my actions, trials, and sufferings,
that my entire being may henceforth only be employed in
loving,
honouring and glorifying Thee.
This is my irrevocable will,
to belong entirely to Thee,
and to do all for Thy love,
renouncing with my whole heart all that can displease
Thee.

I take Thee, O Sacred Heart,

for the sole object of my love,
the protection of my life,
the pledge of my salvation,
the remedy of my frailty and inconstancy,
the reparation for all the defects of my life,
and my secure refuge at the hour of my death.
Be Thou, O Most Merciful Heart,
my justification before God Thy Father,
and screen me from His anger
which I have so justly merited.
I fear all from my own weakness and malice,
but placing my entire confidence in Thee,
O Heart of Love,
I hope all from Thine infinite Goodness.
Annihilate in me all that can displease or resist Thee.
Imprint Thy pure love so deeply in my heart
that I may never forget Thee or be separated from Thee.
I beseech Thee, through Thine infinite Goodness,
grant that my name be engraved upon Thy Heart,
for in this I place all my happiness
and all my glory,
to live and to die as one of Thy devoted servants.

Amen.

Consecration to The Immaculate Heart of Mary

I, (Name), a faithless sinner -
renew and ratify today in thy hands,
O Immaculate Mother,
the vows of my Baptism;
I renounce forever Satan,

his pomps and works;
and I give myself entirely to Jesus Christ,
the Incarnate Wisdom,
to carry my cross after Him
all the days of my life,
and to be more faihful to Him
than I have ever been before.

In the presence of all the heavenly court
I choose thee this day,
for my Mother and Mistress.
I deliver and consecrate to thee,
as thy slave, my body and soul,
my goods, both interior and exterior,
and even the value of all my good actions,
past, present and future;
leaving to thee the entire
and full right of disposing of me,
and all that belongs to me, without exception,
according to thy good pleasure,
for the greater glory of God,
in time and in eternity.

Amen.

Consecration to St Joseph, Patron of the Church

O Blessed Joseph,
Virginal Father of my Savior
and chaste spouse of the mother of God,
this day I irrevocably adopt thee
for my intercessor with the Almighty as well as my model,
my protector and my father in this valley of exile.

O St. Joseph,
whom the Lord constituted guardian of His Family,
I beseech thee to extend thy tender solicitude over all my
interests.
Kindle in my heart a vehement love for Jesus
and enable me to serve Him with all thy devotedness and
fidelity.
Aid my inability to venerate Mary as my advocate,
to honor her as my Queen and to love her as my Mother.
Be my never-failing guide in the way of virtue and piety,
and grant that, after having faithfully followed thee in the
path of justice,
I may receive thy powerful protection at the hour of my
death.
Amen.

Consecration to the Holy Spirit

O Holy Spirit, Divine Spirit of light, life and love; I
consecrate to thee my understanding, heart and will, my
whole being for time and eternity. May my understanding
be always submissive to Thy heavenly inspirations, and to
the teachings of the Holy Catholic Church, of which Thou
art the infallible guide;

May my heart be ever inflamed with love of God and of
my neighbor; may my will be ever more perfectly
conformed to the divine Will, and may my whole life be a
faithful imitation of the life and virtues of our Lord and
Savior, Jesus Christ, to Whom, with the Father and Thee
be honor and Glory forever.

Amen.

Prayer to the Most Holt Trinity

O God, Thou who art one in nature and three in persons,
Father, Son, and Holy Spirit,
first cause and last end of all creatures,
the infinite Good,
incomprehensible and ineffable,
my Creator, my Redeemer, and my Sanctifier,
I believe in Thee,
I hope in Thee,
and I love Thee with all my heart.

In the midst of Thine infinite happiness,
Thou didst choose me,
through no merits of mine,
in preference to countless other creatures,
who would doubtless have corresponded with Thy
blessings better than I have done;
Thou didst love me from eternity;
and when my hour in time had come,
Thou didst draw me from nothingness into earthly
existence
and didst bestow upon me Thy grace,
as a pledge of everlasting life.

From the depths of my misery,
I adore Thee and I give Thee thanks.
Thy holy Name was invoked over my cradle
to be my profession of faith,
my plan of action,
and the only goal of my earthly pilgrimage;

grant, O most Holy Trinity,
that I may ever be inspired by this faith,
and may carry out this plan with perseverance,
so that, when I have reached the end of my journey upon
earth,
I may be able to fix my gaze
upon the blessed splendours of Thy glory.

Amen.

Prayer for the Holy Father

Lord Jesus, shelter our Holy Father, the Pope, under the
protection of thy Sacred Heart. Be Thou his light, his
strength and his consolation.

Prayer of St. Gertrude the Great for the Holy Souls in Purgatory

O Eternal Father,
I offer Thee the most precious Blood of Thy Divine Son,
Jesus,
in union with the Masses said throughout the world today,
for all the holy souls in Purgatory
for sinners everywhere,
for sinners in the Universal Church,
for those in my own home
and for those within my family.

Closing Prayer to St. Michael

Saint Michael the Archangel,
Defend us in battle
Be our protection against the wickedness and snares of the
devil;
May God rebuke him, we humbly pray;
And do thou, O Prince of the heavenly host,
By the power of God, thrust into hell
Satan and all evil spirits
Who wander through the world
For the ruin of souls.

Amen

CHAPTER TEN

DELIVERANCE

Deliverance can be defined as the process of prayerfully driving demons out of a person in the name of Jesus Christ. You may be surprised to learn that, according to Fr. Gabriel Amorth (former chief Exorcist of the Diocese of Rome), even baptized laypersons have the power to "drive out demons." Fr. Amorth bases his conviction on Christ's exhortation to his followers: "Heal the sick, raise the dead, cleanse the lepers, *cast out devils*: freely have you received, freely give" (Mt 10:8).

While all baptized Christians are capable of sharing in Christ's ministry of "driving out demons," very few Christians actually exercise it. This is likely due to the Catholic Church's strong prohibition against laypersons using the official Rite of Exorcism, which is reserved for priests who have been authorized and commissioned by their bishop. Technically, exorcism is a sacramental of the Church, only to be used by validly ordained priests who have the authority to use it. While exorcism is extremely beneficial to those unfortunate souls who may be oppressed, obsessed or possessed by the Devil or demons, it is extremely rare to find a priest or even a bishop who will perform the rite.

There are many reasons exorcism has largely fallen out of popular usage. With the advent of the science of psychology and a better understanding and awareness of psychopathology (mental illness), the Church, as a matter of protocol, must first rule out psychopathology as the true, root cause of the frightening symptoms which appear to mimic demonic possession. However, we must contend with the reality that mental illness and demonic influence are not at all mutually exclusive, which is to say if a person is afflicted with one of these issues, that same individual cannot simultaneously be afflicted with the other. On the contrary, it has been this author's experience, both as a Mental Health Clinician and as a Pastoral Counselor that most persons who present with mental health issues tend to be especially susceptible to demonic attack. This should come as no surprise to anyone, as the devil and his minions are notorious for attacking and exploiting human weaknesses and vulnerabilities. Consequently, it is extremely rare to find individuals who are victims of either pure demonic attack or pure mental illness. The two almost invariably go hand-in-hand.

It is precisely for this reason that I advocate a two-pronged approach that addresses and treats both the mental health component (with a combination of talk therapy and psychopharmacology) and the spiritual component (which employs the use of deliverance prayers, or, in more extreme cases, a Church-sanctioned Exorcism.

It has become this author's belief that many bishops, in deferring to psychiatrists and psychologists when

individuals begin to complain of problems that may or
may not be demonic in origin, are over-relying on the
mental-health profession, much to the detriment of
genuinely agitated souls in desperate need of Church
intervention. To be sure, there are, in fact, mental
disorders which mimic demonic possession. But just
because this is so does not mean that bishops should
always defer to psychological experts, or that true demonic
possession doesn't exist. Demonic harassment is quite
real, and is much more common than people may think.
Thus, the exorcist has a critical role to play in our
increasingly hedonistic, materialistic, narcissistic,
antagonistic, nihilistic and atheistic culture of death.. And
since many bishops have been and continue to be remiss
in their duties by not designating at least one priest-
exorcist per diocese, the task should, in this author's
estimation, be taken up by competent laypersons –
Christian men and women who are devout in the practice
of their faith, and are willing to enter into combat with the
forces of evil.

I should clarify the point that a lay person is *never* to
perform an exorcism, and can never properly label him or
herself an *Exorcist*. But lay persons can and should engage
in ministries of deliverance, which can be just as effective.
Essentially, the exorcist and the lay person involved in
deliverance ministry are doing the same thing; namely,
driving out demons in the most holy name of Jesus Christ,
by the power of His Precious Blood, the price of our
salvation and ransom from the Prince of Darkness. The
difference is that the priest 1. acts in Persona Christi (the
Person of Christ), and 2. exorcises on behalf of the
Church, with the full power and authority of the Church
behind him. Thus, it stands to reason that
exorcism would presumably be more powerful than simple
prayers of deliverance on the part of a lay person. Yet, as
Fr. Amorth rightly points out, the stronger the faith of the

one driving out demons in Christ's name, the better the chance the demon(s) will flee. Thus, deliverance and exorcism are largely dependent upon the faith of the one performing the prayers.

Fr. Amorth gives the example of St. Catherine of Sienna. There was an exorcist-priest who resided in her diocese, and whenever he could not cast a demon out of someone, he would send that individual to St. Catherine. She would pray, and, invariably, the demon(s) would flee and the individual would be liberated. Fr. Amorth points out that St. Catherine was neither a priest nor an exorcist, but she was a saint! Thus, we should never underestimate the power of faith in the process of deliverance.

While lay men and women are not permitted to use the official Rite of Exorcism, there are very effective prayers of deliverance that can be used. Individuals like Neal Lozano have, after years of deliverance ministry, put forth methodical procedures to adhere to when attempting to deliver an individual from the influence of an evil spirit or spirits. Lozano's technique is based on years of experience as a deliverance minister, and has proven to be most effective when carried out by a faith-filled Christian who knows him or herself to be in a state of sanctifying grace.

For the sake of releasing those poor, afflicted souls that are oppressed, obsessed or possessed, I shall provide here the five-step method (The Unbound Method of Deliverance) proposed for use by Lozano and found in its entirety in his book, "Unbound: A Practical Guide to Deliverance," Moreover, in conjunction with Lozano's tried and true methods, I shall provide additional excellent resources that I, personally, have found to be most efficacious in my own deliverance ministry. It is my conviction that, if applied correctly, the guidelines set forth below will surely release any persons who may be under the influence of evil, demonic spirits.

*An important note to the deliverance minister: Please be certain that you, yourself, make a good, thorough confession to a validly ordained Catholic priest before you attempt to engage in any type of deliverance on behalf of anyone. Engaging in this type of ministry can be extremely dangerous if one is not properly spiritually prepared. The best preparation is to know that you are in a state of sanctifying grace. It is also extremely beneficial to set aside a significant amount of time for prayer and fasting before you attempt to deliver a soul from the clutches of the evil one; the deliverance minister is playing on the Devil's turf, and the devil isn't too happy about that. Without the proper spiritual preparation, you could very well put yourself and your own soul at risk of be attacked, harassed, or worse. Thus, it is the advice of this author to the deliverance minister that he/she take every possible precaution, including, but not limited to: intense prayer (especially the Holy Rosary); fasting (bread and water); recourse to the Sacrament of penance/Reconciliation; reception of the most holy Eucharist; use of holy, blessed and/or exorcised water/oil/salt and use of the Benedictine Crucifix during the deliverance sessions.

Process of Deliverance

1. **Prayer for forgiveness.** Pray with the afflicted person for the forgiveness of any and all sin. The person must be truly repentant, and must be ready and able to forgive everyone who has harmed him/her. Ideally, have the person avail themselves of the sacrament of confession before any deliverance prayer is performed. In many cases, the demon(s) will be driven out in the sacrament of penance itself. In fact, confession is the "normal" method of ridding a person of demonic influence. If, after a good, exhaustive confession, the individual is still feeling

harassed, proceed with the following.
2. Pray the Long Version of the **Exorcism Prayer of St. Michael**, composed by Pope Leo XIII:

O glorious Archangel St. Michael, Prince of the heavenly host, defend us in battle, and in the struggle which is ours against the principalities and Powers, against the rulers of this world of darkness, against spirits of evil in high places (Eph 6:12). Come to the aid of men, whom God created immortal, made in his own image and likeness, and redeemed at a great price from the tyranny of the devil (Wis 2:23-24, 1 Cor 6:20).

Fight this day the battle of the Lord, together with the holy angels, as already thou hast fought the leader of the proud angels, Lucifer, and his apostate host, who were powerless to resist thee, nor was there place for them any longer in Heaven. But that cruel, that ancient serpent, who is called the devil or Satan, who seduces the whole world, was cast into the abyss with all his angels (Rev 12:7-9).

Behold, this primeval enemy and slayer of man has taken courage, Transformed into an angel of light, he wanders about with all the multitude of wicked spirits, invading the earth in order to blot out the name of God and of his Christ, to seize upon, slay and cast into eternal perdition souls destined for the crown of eternal glory. This wicked dragon pours out, as a most impure flood, the venom of his malice on men of depraved mind and corrupt heart, the spirit of lying, of impiety, of blasphemy, and the pestilent breath of impurity, and of every vice and iniquity.

These most crafty enemies have filled and inebriated with gall and bitterness the Church, the spouse of the Immaculate Lamb, and have laid impious hands on her most sacred possessions (Lam 3:15).
In the Holy Place itself, where has been set up the See of the most holy Peter and the Chair of Truth for the light of the world, they have raised the throne of their abominable impiety, with the iniquitous design that when the Pastor has been struck, the sheep may be scattered.

Arise then, O invincible prince, bring help against the attacks of the lost spirits to the people of God, and bring them the victory.

The Church venerates thee as protector and patron; in thee holy Church glories as her defense against the malicious powers of this world and of hell; to thee has God entrusted the souls of men to be established in heavenly beatitude.

Oh, pray to the God of peace that He may put Satan under our feet, so far conquered that he may no longer be able to hold men in captivity and harm the Church. Offer our prayers in the sight of the Most High, so that they may quickly conciliate the mercies of the Lord; and beating down the dragon, the ancient serpent, who is the devil and Satan, do thou again make him captive in the abyss, that he may no longer seduce the nations. Amen.

L: Behold the Cross of the Lord; be scattered ye hostile powers.
R. The Lion of the Tribe of Judah has conquered the root of David.
L. Let Thy mercies be upon us, O Lord.
R. As we have hoped in Thee.
L. O Lord, hear my prayer.
R. And let my cry come unto Thee.
L. Let us pray:

O God, the Father of Our Lord Jesus Christ, we call upon Thy Holy Name, and as supplicants we implore thy clemency, that by the intercession of Mary, ever Virgin, Immaculate and Our Mother, and of the glorious St. Michael the Archangel, Thou wouldst deign to help us against Satan and all the other unclean spirits, who wander about the world for the injury of the human race and the ruin of souls. Amen.

3. Pray the **Litany of the Saints**:

Lord, have mercy,
Christ, have mercy.

Lord, have mercy,
Christ, hear us.
Christ, graciously hear us.
God, the Father of Heaven,   have mercy on us.
God, the Redeemer of the world,   have mercy on us.
God, the Holy Spirit,   have mercy on us.
Holy Trinity, one God,   have mercy on us.
Holy Mary,   pray for us.
Holy Virgin of Virgins,   pray for us.
St. Michael,   pray for us.
St. Gabriel,   pray for us.
St. Raphael,   pray for us.
All holy angels and archangels,   pray for us.
All holy orders of blessed spirits,   pray for us.
St. John the Baptist,   pray for us.
St. Joseph,   pray for us.
All holy patriarchs and prophets,   pray for us.
St. Peter,   pray for us.
St. Paul,   pray for us.
St. Andrew,   pray for us.
St. James,   pray for us.
St. John,   pray for us.

St. Thomas,	pray for us.
St. Philip,	pray for us.
St. Bartholomew,	pray for us.
St. Matthew,	pray for us
.St. Simon,	pray for us.
St. Thaddeus,	pray for us.
St. Matthias,	pray for us.
St. Barnabas,	pray for us.
St. Luke,	pray for us.
St. Mark,	pray for us.
All holy apostles and evangelists,	pray for us.
All holy disciples of the Lord,	pray for us.
All holy innocents,	pray for us.
St. Stephen,	pray for us.
St. Lawrence,	pray for us.
St. Vincent,	pray for us.
SS. Fabian and Sebastian,	pray for us.
SS. John and Paul,	pray for us.
SS. Cosmos and Damian,	pray for us.
SS. Gervase and Protase,	pray for us.

All Holy Martyrs,	pray for us.
St. Sylvester,	pray for us.
St. Ambrose,	pray for us.
St. Augustine,	pray for us.
St. Jerome,	pray for us.
St. Martin,	pray for us.
St. Nicholas,	pray for us.
All holy bishops and confessors,	pray for us.
All holy doctors,	pray for us.
St. Anthony,	pray for us.
St. Benedict,	pray for us.
St. Bernard,	pray for us.
St. Francis,	pray for us.
All holy priests and Levites,	pray for us.
All holy monks and hermits,	pray for us.
St. Mary Magdalen,	pray for us.
St. Agatha,	pray for us.
St. Lucy,	pray for us.
St. Agnes,	pray for us.
St. Cecelia,	pray for us.
St. Catherine,	pray for us.
St. Anastasia,	pray for

us.

All holy virgins and windows,	pray for us.
All holy saints of God,	intercede for us.
Be merciful,	spare us, O Lord.
Be merciful,	graciously hear us, O Lord.
From all evil,	deliver us, O Lord.
From all sin,	deliver us, O Lord.
From your wrath,	deliver us, O Lord.
From sudden and provided death,	deliver us, O Lord.
From the snare of the devil,	deliver us, O Lord.
From anger, hatred , and all ill will,	deliver us, O Lord.
From all lewdness,	deliver us, O Lord.
From lightning and tempest,	deliver us, O Lord.
From the scourage of earthquakes,	deliver us, O Lord.

From the plague, famine, and war, deliver us, O Lord.

From everlasting death, deliver us, O Lord.

By the mystery of your holy incarnation, deliver us, O Lord. By your coming, deliver us, O Lord.

By your birth, deliver us, O Lord.

By your baptism and holy fasting, deliver us, O Lord.

By your cross and passion, deliver us, O Lord.

By your holy resurrection, deliver us, O Lord.

By your wondrous ascension, deliver us, O Lord.

By the coming of the Holy Spirit, the Advocate, deliver us,

O Lord.

On the day of judgement, deliver us, O Lord.

We sinners, we beg you to hear us.

That you spare us,

That you pardon us,

That you bring us to true penance,

That you govern and preserve your holy Church,

That you preserve our Holy Father,

and all ranks in the Church in holy religion,

That you humble the enemies of the holy Church,

That you give peace and true concord to all Christian rulers, That you give peace and unity to the whole Christian world, That you restore to the unity of the Church all who have strayed from the truth, and lead all unbelievers to the light of the Gospel,

That you confirm and preserve us in your hold service,

That you lift up our minds to heavenly desires,

That you grant everlasting blessings to all our benefactors,

That you deliver our souls and the souls of our brethren, relatives, and benefactors from everlasting damnation,

That you give and preserve the fruits of the earth,

That you grant eternal rest to all the faithful departed,

That you graciously hear us, Son of God.

Lamb of God, who takes away the sins of the world, spare us, O Lord.

Lamb of God, who takes away the sins of the world, spare us, O Lord.

Lamb of God, who takes away the sins of the world, have mercy on us.

Christ, hear us,

Christ, graciously hear us.

Lord, have mercy.

Christ have mercy.

Lord have mercy.

Let us pray.

From You, Lord come holiness in our desires, right thinking in our plans, and justice in our actions. Grant Your children the peace which the world cannot give; then our hearts will be devoted to Your laws, we shall be delivered from the terrors of war, and under Your protection we shall be able to Live in tranquility. Amen.

4. **Renunciation**. Have the person (1) *renounce* each area of bondage and (2) *bind* the wicked, demonic spirits, all in the name of Jesus. For example, you might use the following words: *"In the name of Jesus I renounce and bind the spirits of lust. In the name of Jesus, I renounce and bind the spirits of pride, etc."*

It is important that the individual first identify the areas of bondage and that he or she personally renounce these spirits. You, as the deliverance minister, can lead the person in the renunciation process, especially if the person is timid, shy, or just uncomfortable. To be sure that you have renounced all possible areas of bondage, I shall here reproduce a fairly exhaustive and comprehensive list of common areas of bondage to be renounced, should they apply. Since it is far better to err on the side of caution, it is a good idea to simply renounce and bind every one of the possible areas of bondage listed:

"Envy, criticism, impatience, resentment, pride, rebellion, stubbornness, unforgiveness, gossip, disobedience, strife, violence, divorce, accusation, anger, manipulation, jealousy, greed, laziness, revenge, coveting, possessiveness, control, retaliation, selfishness, deceitfulness, deception, dishonesty, unbelief, seduction, lust, pornography, masturbation, idolatry, witchcraft, physical and psychological infirmities, nerve disorder, lung disorder, brain disorder or dysfunction, AIDS, cancer, hypochondriasis, hyperactivity, depression, schizophrenia, fatigue, anorexia, bulimia, addictions, gluttony, perfectionism, alcoholism, self-abuse, sexual addictions, sexual perversions, attempted suicide, incest, pedophilia, lesbianism, homosexuality, adultery, homophobia, confusion, ignorance, procrastination, self-hatred, isolation, loneliness, ostracism, paranoia, nervousness, passivity, indecision, doubt, oppression, rejection, poor self-image, anxiety, shame, timidity, fear, and finally, each of the seven deadly sins and everything that leads to a failure to love God with all of one's heart, soul, strength and mind, and a everything that leads to a failure to love one's brothers and sisters as Christ has loved us."

Be sure not to forget to have the individual renounce any authority over his/her life that he/she might have given inadvertently to a soothsayer, a psychic, fortune-teller, etc, by stating, *"In the name of Jesus I renounce the authority over my life I gave to (name of fortune-teller),and to the spirit that operated in (name)."* Bondage can additionally be the result of sexual unions the person has had outside of the context of marriage. Such bondage is referred to as a soul-tie. In this instance, have the person say, *"In the name of Jesus, I renounce all sexual and spiritual bondage to (name of person), and I take back the authority I gave to him/her."*

5. **Take authority**. This is where spiritual confrontation and combat occur. Pray over the afflicted person using the following formula: "In the name of Jesus I break and dissolve the power of every spirit that (name) has renounced and any related spirit, and I command them now to leave in the name of Jesus, to depart quietly, without manifestation or harm to anyone, and I command you to go straight to Jesus, and to the foot of His cross, for Him to deal with you as He sees fit." You, as a deliverance minister, may want to have the afflicted person speak the words of command for him or herself. Either way, this is the crux of the deliverance.

6. **Pray the Litany of Holy Command**:

Re-printed with permission from: http://thewarriorprince.
wordpress.com/michael-and-the-litany-of-holycommand/:

The Litany of Holy Command, a deliverance prayer, was
given in recent years by Archangel Michael, for use by any
of the faithful in a state of grace (Nwoye, B. 2009. *The
breeze of the Second Pentecost*). Following are Michael's words
regarding the Litany and the prayer itself:

"I come to give you the 'Litany of Holy Command,' which
you have as a Catholic, but many of you do not know . . .
Mortal man, you have the Holy Mass, the greatest prayer
on earth. You have your Rosary, the Chaplet of the
Precious Blood, and all the devotional prayers of the
Church. These are the great prayers that have power over
the hosts of demons. With these prayers, your authorities
as a child of God, and this 'Litany of Holy Command,' a
mortified child of God will drive away any type of demon
from whatever level" (Archangel Michael).

The Litany of Holy Command

I command you, whoever you may be, unclean spirits,
wicked spirits of Hell, to give place to the Holy Spirit of
God, Who owns this/these Temple(s).
Deliver us (him/her), O Lord, by the Power of Your Holy Name.

In the Name and by the Power of the True God, the Holy
God, and the Only Living God.

Deliver us (him/her), O Lord, by the Power of Your Holy Name.

I command you, in the Name of Our Lord Jesus Christ to
leave this/these Temple(s) and return to the abyss.

Deliver us (him/her), O Lord, by the Power of Your Holy Name.

In the Name of the Precious Blood of the Spotless Lamb of God, I command you.

Deliver us (him/her), O Lord, by the Power of Your Holy Name.

In the Name of the Holy Ghost, I command you.

Deliver us (him/her), O Lord, by the Power of Your Holy Name.

In the Name of Holy Mary, who crushed your head, I command you.

Deliver us (him/her), O Lord, by the Power of Your Holy Name.

Her Immaculate Conception commands you.

Deliver us (him/her), O Lord, by the Power of Your Holy Name.

Her Virginity and Purity command you.

Deliver us (him/her), O Lord, by the Power of Your Holy Name.

Her holy Obedience, Patience, and Humility command you.

Deliver us (him/her), O Lord, by the Power of Your Holy Name.
Her Heart, pierced with the swords of Sorrows, commands you.

Deliver us (him/her), O Lord, by the Power of Your Holy Name.

Her glorious Assumption commands you.

Deliver us (him/her), O Lord, by the Power of Your Holy Name.

Depart! You infernal spirits, in the Name of Mary; Queen

of Heaven and earth.

Deliver us (him/her), O Lord, by the Power of Your Holy Name.

In the Name of the Holy, Catholic, and Apostolic Church; I command you.

Deliver us (him/her), O Lord, by the Power of Your Holy Name.

The faith of Peter and Paul and of all the Apostles commands you.

Deliver us (him/her), O Lord, by the Power of Your Holy Name.
The blood of Martyrs commands you.

Deliver us (him/her), O Lord, by the Power of Your Holy Name.

The purity of Virgins and of all the Saints commands you.

Deliver us (him/her), O Lord, by the Power of Your Holy Name.

Be gone, you wicked legions, in the Name of the Holy Catholic Faith.

Deliver us (him/her), O Lord, by the Power of Your Holy Name.

In the Name and by the Power of the Eucharistic Jesus Christ present in the Tabernacles all over the world, I command you.

Deliver us (him/her), O Lord, by the Power of Your Holy Name.

The Sacred Chalice, which contains the Precious Blood of Jesus Christ commands you.

Deliver us (him/her), O Lord, by the Power of Your Holy Name.

The Sacred Sign of the Cross commands you.

Deliver us (him/her), O Lord, by the Power of Your Holy Name.

Flee, you disobedient, by the merits of the Holy Wounds of Our Lord Jesus Christ.

Deliver us (him/her), O Lord, by the Power of Your Holy Name.

In the Name of God, the Father Almighty, and by the obedience of His Angels, I command you.

Deliver us (him/her), O Lord, by the Power of Your Holy Name.

The Celestial Choirs of Seraphim and Cherubim command you.

Deliver us (him/her), O Lord, by the Power of Your Holy Name.

The Celestial Choirs of Thrones and Dominions command you.

Deliver us (him/her), O Lord, by the Power of Your Holy Name.

The Celestial Choirs of Powers and Virtues command you.

Deliver us (him/her), O Lord, by the Power of Your Holy Name.
The Celestial Choir of Principalities commands you.

Deliver us (him/her), O Lord, by the Power of Your Holy Name.

The Celestial Choir of Angels commands you.

Deliver us (him/her), O Lord, by the Power of Your Holy Name.

The Celestial Choir of Archangels commands you.

BECOMING AN APOSTLE OF LIGHT OF THE IMMACULATE HEART OF MARY

Deliver us (him/ her), O Lord, by the Power of Your Holy Name.

O God of Heaven and earth, God of Angels and Archangels, Who is like Thee? I beg You to rebuke these wicked spirits by the Power of Your Holy Name.

Deliver us (him/ her), O Lord, by the Power of Your Holy Name.

Jesus, the Son of the ever-Virgin, I adore Your Blood of Circumcision and beseech You to deliver us by Your Precious Blood.

Deliver us by Your Precious Blood.

Jesus, the only begotten Son of God, by Your Sweat of Blood,

Deliver us by Your Precious Blood.

Jesus, the Sacrificial Lamb, by Your Scourging,

Deliver us by Your Precious Blood.

Jesus, crowned with Thorns,

Deliver us by Your Precious Blood.

Jesus, Who carried the Cross for our Salvation,

Deliver us by Your Precious Blood.

Jesus Crucified,

Deliver us by Your Precious Blood.

Jesus, pierced on the Side from which Blood and Water come out,

Deliver us by Your Precious Blood.

Jesus, I beseech You to save us. Amen.

Let us pray:

O God, set Your children free who are possessed by the powers of darkness + In the Name of the Father + and of the Son + and of the Holy Spirit. Amen.

(Source: *The breeze of the Second Pentecost,* pp. 145-149).

7. Prayer of thanksgiving. Once it is clear that the person has been set free, pray in thanksgiving to Jesus: " *Thank you, Jesus, for setting (name) free. Thank you, Jesus, for releasing him/her from the bondage to (name area of bondage)."*

8. **Prayer of Blessing**. Pray that the newly freed individual might be blessed anew in the Holy Spirit. You might use the following words: "Come, Holy Spirit. Come by the means of the most powerful intercession of the Immaculate Heart of Mary, your well-beloved spouse, and fill this person with your many gifts and blessings. Please fill up any areas that have been left vacant by the departure of evil spirits. Fill any and all vacancies with the love, the joy, the peace, healing and light of the Risen Lord Jesus Christ. We now ask you to bless and seal (name) in the blood of Jesus Christ, the price of our salvation."

9. **Re-dedication and re-consecration of this living temple to the Divine Will of God the Father, to the Precious Blood of Jesus, and to the Sacred Hearts of Jesus and Mary.** Any number of solemn acts of consecration may be made to Jesus through Mary. The following prayer of Consecration is most effective in the re-dedication and re-consecration of the Lord's Living

Temple to Jesus through Mary:

Act of Consecration to the Sacred Heart of Jesus through the Immaculate Heart of Mary in the Spirit of St. Joseph

Hail, Holy Queen of Heaven and earth, Refuge of Sinners, Woman clothed with the Sun (cf. Rev 12:1), Virgin of Fatima, Spouse of the Holy Spirit, our Spiritual Mother (cf. Jn 19:26) and Mediatrix of all Grace and Mercy; we, the Apostles of Light of Your Immaculate Heart, come before you this day to renew, through, with and in your Immaculate Heart, the solemn vows made at our baptism. We firmly reject Satan, the ancient serpent (cf. Rev 12:9), the Father of Lies, and a murderer from the beginning (cf. Jn 8:44), whose head, swollen with pride, shall be crushed beneath your heel (cf. Gen 3:15), and of whose poison cup we refuse to drink; we reject this world and its vanities, of which the devil is prince (cf. Jn 12:31); finally, we reject every form of impurity of mind, body and spirit.

In the presence of the most high Triune God and His cloud of heavenly witnesses (cf. Heb 12:1-2), the angels and saints, we take you, O Blessed Virgin Mary, as our Spiritual Mother (cf. Jn 19:26); and we hereby espouse your Immaculate Heart (cf. Sir 15:1-2), that, in imitation of St. Joseph and under his fatherly protection, our hearts might beat in a perfect union of love with and for the most Sacred and Eucharistic Heart of Jesus, the Christ, for all time and eternity. Moreover, through our mutual exchange of hearts, O sweetest Queen Mother, may the Triumph of your Immaculate Heart take place in our souls.

Furthermore, O gracious Virgin, we pray that you might nourish our parched souls with the milk of divine grace. May our hearts, like yours, blossom into lush gardens of heavenly delights, virtues and graces, and become fitting temples for your divine Spouse, the most Holy Spirit of God (cf. 1 Cor 3:16), thereby grafting and uniting us ever more perfectly to the Mystical Body of Christ (cf. 1 Cor 12:12) and reproducing in our souls the image of Christ crucified.

Thus, we solemnly entrust and consecrate to you, O Immaculate Virgin Mary, in our abject misery, poverty, weakness, sinfulness and nothingness, everything that we are and have, just as we are, without reserve: body, soul, intellect, will and emotions; all of our interior and exterior goods and possessions; and even the satisfactory, meritorious value of all our good works – past, present and future – for you to dispose of according to the designs of your Immaculate Heart, in anticipation of the promised Triumph of your Immaculate Heart in the Church and the world and the long-awaited establishment of the holy city, the new Jerusalem, that shall come down out of heaven, and in which Christ shall establish His glorious Eucharistic reign of peace, justice, holiness and love (cf. Rev 21:2).

Like a lamb led to the slaughter who opens not his mouth (cf. Acts 8:32), we place ourselves and the spiritual sacrifices of our prayers, works and especially the sufferings of this day and of our entire lives on the consecrated altar of your Immaculate Heart. Please unite each one of us and our offerings to Jesus' spotless and unblemished offering of Himself to the perfect glorification of the Eternal Father, renewed this day and every day, from the rising of the sun to its setting, in the Most Holy Sacrifice of the Mass. We make this offering in atonement for the sins of our whole lives and for those of the whole world, in a profound act of glorification, adoration, gratitude, expiation and supplication to the Most Holy Trinity, for the intentions of the Two

Sacred Hearts of Jesus and Mary, for the Church's solemn recognition and definition of Your Spiritual Motherhood, Mary, as the "Co-Redemptrix, Mediatrix and Advocate," and for the conversion, sanctification and salvation of all souls until the end of time.

In imitation of Christ, your dearly beloved Son, "the firstborn of all creation" (cf. Col 1:15), we humbly request that the chalice of suffering might be taken from us (cf. Lk 22:42); yet, with Christ and in imitation of you, O Holy Virgin, we ultimately submit our unconditional and irrevocable *fiat* to the Divine Will of the Eternal Father as we state, "Behold the servant of the Lord; be it done to me according to thy word" (cf. Lk 1:38); and we patiently accept, in advance, whatever crosses and sufferings that the Divine Heart of God the Father chooses to send us (cf. Lk 1:38). O Mother and Mediatrix of all Grace and Mercy, may we truly participate in Your fullness of Grace and be clothed with your own heroic faith, hope, charity, purity, humility, fortitude, and that perfect resignation of will necessary to deny our very selves, pick up our crosses daily, and follow Jesus (cf. Lk 9:23) on the narrow path of evangelical poverty, chastity and obedience; bearing witness to our faith in Christ and His Holy Gospel in all of our thoughts, words and deeds, even to the point of the shedding of our blood, should we be called to wear the holy crown of martyrdom.

And when our mission on this earth has been accomplished, we pray that, as the littlest of your many children and the smallest flowers in the Garden of your Immaculate Heart, you Mary, along with your Divine Son Jesus, might be present at our side with your glorified bodies to receive our dying breath and to escort our souls straight to the throne of the Thrice Holy Godhead; that the Eternal Father, seeing reproduced in our souls the image of His crucified Christ, might invite us to the Eternal Banquet, the heavenly wedding feast of the Lamb and His Bride, the Church (cf. Rev 19:9). Furthermore, having comprised the humble "heel" of the Mystical Body used by you, Mary, to crush the head of the ancient serpent (cf. Gen: 3:15), may we, one day, make up bright, shining stars in the crown about your Most Immaculate Heart (cf. Rev 12:1). And may we behold He Who is, Who was, and Who shall be for all eternity, participating in the merits of the angels and saints in paradise and in the eternal chorus of praise, glory, wisdom, thanks, honor, power and might to our God forever and forever (cf. Rev 7:12). Amen.

After the deliverance has taken place, the deliverance minister should offer some prayers to be protected against any spirits seeking revenge on him or her for doing the Lord's work. The devil will be angry that you have released a soul from his captivity and may desire to attack the deliverance minister. To avoid this, claim the Precious, shed blood of Jesus over all aspects of your life, ministry, airspace, sources of supply, your physical, psychological and spiritual health and wellbeing. Further, ask the Blessed Mother to intercede for both you and the one who has just been delivered, that she might shield you both from the snares and the attacks of the enemy by enfolding you and the one Jesus delivered through you in her Immaculate Heart and covering you with her Immaculate mantle of protection, holiness and purity.

ABOUT THE AUTHOR

Jayson M. Brunelle, M.Ed., CAGS, holds a Bachelor of Arts in Philosophy and Theology from Franciscan University of Steubenville, a Master of Education in Counseling Psychology from Springfield College and a Certificate of Advanced Graduate Studies in Clinical Mental Health Counseling, also from Springfield College. Moreover, Brunelle earned a Certificate of Completion from the Pre-Theology program at St. John's Seminary, School of Theology. Brunelle has come full-circle, academically speaking, as he is currently working toward a second Master's degree in Theology at Franciscan University. Brunelle's writings have been featured in the "Homiletic and Pastoral Review" and "Lay Witness," and have been listed among "The Best in Catholic Blogging" by EWTN's "National Catholic Register." Recently, he became the Host of the Catholic Internet-Based Radio Show, *Glories of Mary*, which aires live, every Thursday evening, from 8:00 PM to 9:00 PM, on http://www.wcatradio.com, the on-air wing of En Route Media, founded by Dr. Sebastian Mahfood. Brunelle's blog is www.MarianApostolate.com, and he may be reached at jaymbru@gmail.com.